DESIGN ACTIVITIES FOR THE CLASSROOM

JOHN LIDSTONE

Davis Publications, Inc. / Worcester, Massachusetts

DESIGN ACTIVITIES FOR THE CLASSROOM

17

Photographs by ROGER KERKHAM

Printing: Davis Press, Inc.
Binding: Halliday Lithograph
Type: Optima
Graphic Design: Margaret Ong Tsao

10 9 8 7 6 5 4 3 2 1

Preface

Design Activities for the Classroom is an expanded revision of Design Activities for the Elementary Classroom first published some fourteen years ago. While research in art education and the introduction of new media have undoubtedly helped to upgrade current practice in some schools, most teachers face the same classroom problems they did when Design Activities first appeared. Now as then, the author analyzes the structure of design activity to provide insights and strategies that help teachers develop art programs which circumvent such problems and so are more effective.

The text concentrates on two troublesome aspects of art teaching in the elementary and junior high school grades: large classes and the preadolescent's sudden drift away from free and unself-conscious self-expression. It explores the nature of materials and the organization of creative processes in the development of design activities in which it has been found preadolescents will participate with the same enthusiasm and inventiveness they once approached image making and creative play with paints and clay.

In Design Activities for the Classroom each project has been built around a technique, a process, or a material experience has shown will capture the imagination of the elementary or junior high school student. Each activity consists of several easily understood steps designed to hold the interest of the group. Each activity leaves youngsters free to develop their ideas in open-ended ways that accommodate the abilities and enthusiasms of each individual.

Acknowledgments

The author is grateful to the following persons and organizations for their cheerful cooperation and help:

Alex de Laszlo and Courtney Ward, Collegiate School, New York City; Allan Frumkin Gallery, Chicago; The Brooklyn Museum, Brooklyn; Grace Sayers and J. H. Wainright (principal), Queen Mary School, Vancouver, B.C., Canada; Grace George Alexander-Greene, Assistant Director of Art, New York City Schools; Melissa Weiner; Murray Greenberg; Nathan Lerner; The Museum of Modern Art, New York City and Van Nostrand Reinhold Co. for the use of material from *Creative Movement for Children* (Weiner and Lidstone), page 16 and *Building with Cardboard* (Lidstone), page 41.

Contents

Children have an innate desire to manipulate materials and a seemingly inborn ability to organize them aesthetically in real space or within the two-dimensional plane. One has only to observe young children working with paints or clay or involved in block building or sand and water play to be convinced of this. It is in such activities that we can discern the early evidence of what such authors as Gaitskill and Hurwitz refer to as the child's "design sense."

Everyone has a need for self-expression to reinforce the concept of *self* by reassuring personal statements of one kind or another. Children identify easily with materials and processes. They soon discover that by working directly with them they can make such statements through design. Consequently, they find satisfaction in design activities and are drawn to design as a means of expression.

School art programs should demonstrate both an awareness of this enthusiasm and an appreciation of the child's natural abilities in design. At all levels, the child's originality and inventiveness should be respected and encouraged. Emphasis should be placed on the development of strong personalized statements rather than on formal learning. Activities should grow straight out of challenging processes and stimulating materials. They should be based on a firm intent to preserve and strengthen the child's intuitive feelings for such elements of design as spatial organization.

1

DESIGN IN NATURE

The artist has traditionally turned to nature for inspiration. Rich in colors and textures, consistent yet never monotonous, nature provides the prototype of every conceivable form of human aesthetic expression. The further we depart from the order and beauty exemplified in nature, the more decadent and squalid our environment. The more we abide by the example of nature, the happier the human condition.

In nature, too, we find the roots of our aesthetic responses. Our feelings for order as well as our distaste for monotony stem from natural experience. Even when we examine nature with the highest power microscope we

2

discover constancy of form invariably relieved by nuances of color, graduations of texture, or subtle changes in organization.

Too often, unfortunately, in our preoccupation with everyday affairs, we disregard the abundant wonders of art in nature. For most of us, it takes a vacation in the country, a hiking trip, or, perhaps, the lively interest of a friend to awaken our enthusiasms. Children need to be alerted, just as we do, to the excitement and delights of nature. Once their enthusiasm is aroused, however, some sort of strategy is needed to concentrate their attentions on those aspects of nature having the most to offer in terms of art.

If you have ever sat down with brush, paper, and easel to organize what is to become a composition painted from nature, you will understand that the problem for the painter is not what to include but what to leave out. The teacher has much the same problem, how to focus the child's attention on what is most pertinent in nature at a particular time. This is where devices that exclude extraneous information, such as an inexpensive microscope, a magnifying glass, or even a sheet of cardboard with a small square cut from the center can be of particular importance for art in the classroom. If we take the cardboard and place it over one of the panels on page 2, we will see how it can pinpoint the child's visual perception. Expeditions for collecting specific speci-

mens involve children in the larger view of nature and encourage them to zero in on a particular aspect at the same time. Materials gathered in this way may be used for classroom observation or the actual construction of design projects. A collection of pebbles, for example, is easy to maintain, and, even with any amount of handling, will last forever.

Helping children to discover design through nature provides a means of clarifying what is meant by design without resorting to the use of examples of adult design. This leaves the way clear for children to come up with design ideas that are in every way their own. Looking at and handling shells, for example, is an experience that allows children to identify with the physical aspects of design (organization, shape, color, texture) in a way not possible through slides or photographs. Such physical experiences may be heightened by blindfolding children to accentuate the textures of natural surfaces or by using a flashlight or photographer's spotlight to dramatize form and shape. Observing actual nature materials with regard to design involves a consideration of the relationship of form to function. This relationship, in turn, suggests a logical way to integrate art and design with other subject areas. A seed pod, for instance, is an example of good design, both from the way it functions and because of its aesthetic qualities; so we have a link between art and science (botany).

DESIGN IN THE ENVIRONMENT

Conditioned to life in today's impersonal world of glass, concrete and steel, we are often conscious of only the most evident elements of our environment. Sometimes we are aware and appreciative of its more dramatic aspects, a brilliant sunset, perhaps, or the lights of the

Cakes in Window, Nathan Lerner, 1938.

city at night. Too often, however, in the fast pace of twentieth-century living, we are oblivious to the beauty and character of the commonplace elements of our surroundings.

Even the country child who once poked along country lanes on the way to school is now whisked there by bus, and so is denied one opportunity to observe nature at first hand. Similarly, buses, subways, and trains and the admonitions of parents not to dawdle on dangerous streets hurry city youngsters to school and back. Such restrictive circumstances plus long hours before the television set effectively separate today's students from the environment and minimize whatever time they might spend in the scrutiny of its elements. Obviously, unless the teacher makes an organized effort, few students are likely to realize that their immediate surroundings are rich in striking examples of both incidental and planned design. Once the effort is made, however, the rewards can be considerable.

We do not have to go far afield to unearth design sources that yield not only abundant sensory experiences but content material and motivation for follow-up activities as well. Within minutes of any classroom, students will discover fascinating textures and design forms they had failed to notice even though they pass close by them on their daily journeys to and from school. Familiar sights which before had no design meaning — for example, a store window, a wall of peeling movie posters, or even cracks in the sidewalk — take on fresh significance when the teacher draws attention to them.

Tactile experiences invariably heighten visual concepts of surfaces. Our fingertips can often tell us more about a texture than our eyes. A worm-eaten plank or rust-eroded metal door may be merely symbols of urban decay to the casual passer-by. But they can become objects of interest and aesthetic worth to the child who uses both sight and touch to explore their possibilities. Such close scrutiny of real-life elements in the environment awakens the child's awareness to the worth of materials for their own sake. It also helps free the child from a stereotyped scale of values as to what is beautiful and, therefore, worthy of respect, and what is not.

As in the exploration of all design-related materials and situations, children will have a more rewarding experience if they are engaged in an activity that helps focus their attention. Using crayon, chalk, soft pencil or pastel, and a not too stiff sheet of paper they can make rubbings of the random textures of walls, sidewalks, boards, bark, and screening and the more organized surfaces of embossed signs, manhole covers, grates, carved and molded decorations, and tiles. Foil, papier-mâché, plaster of Paris, clay, and plasticine will pick up the reverse images and textures of many of these surfaces. In some cases, they can then be cast in plaster to reproduce the positive facsimile. Clay pressed into different textures can then be inked and printed. Crayon and pencil rubbings can be amalgamated into texture panels or mounted individually.

Actual materials from the environment can be the basis for effective design activities. Mosaics can be composed of broken tiles, glass, bottle caps, or pebbles. Found materials are excellent as the basis of a sand casting or assemblage. With today's effective adhesives, sculpture can be constructed from discarded machine parts, old springs, bits of wood and fiber as well as from plastic packaging and styrofoam. With good design and selectivity, the flotsam and jetsam of the environment can be put to good use in the construction of strikingly handsome sculpture.

Close scrutiny of natural and fabricated materials can alert children to their art potential and aesthetic worth but a broader look is necessary if they are to appreciate the context in which these elements exist. Now is the time to put away the magnifying glass and the microscope and consider the advantages of the still camera, the pinhole camera, the Polaroid, the Super-8 camera, portable video equipment, and the tape recorder — all of which can be put to good use, even by quite young children. Sketching and other types of

visual record keeping might be attempted. Whatever approach, documentation of any kind not only helps focus attention, it assumes that back in school the results will be projected, displayed, discussed or circulated. This, in turn, suggests that whatever the physical encounter with the environment has been, it will be the prelude to activity in the classroom, so that understanding is reinforced.

One can often discover a wealth of resource material near the school. The design and lettering of signs, as shown on page 6, for example,

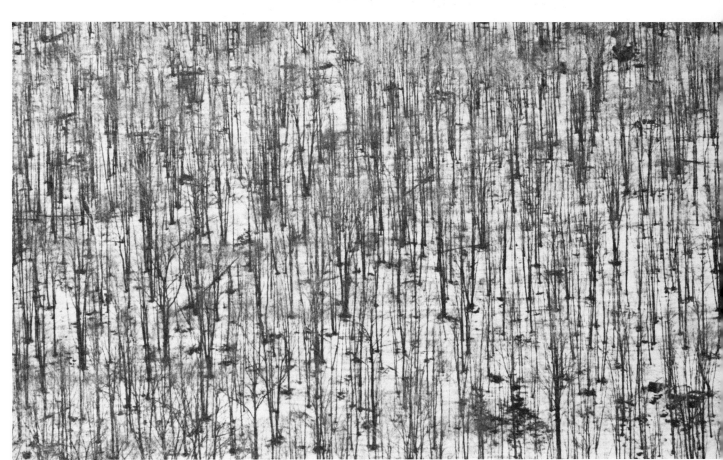

Saplings, Murray Greenberg, 1976.

could be the excuse for a walking tour of a nearby commercial district. A visit to a crafts studio or a factory, or an interview with a local merchant might reveal the significance of design in the life of the community. Neighborhood houses are bound to present a rich assortment of architectural detail and building styles. No matter what the undertaking, student interest will be intensified if there is an exciting task or activity built into it.

When we analyze the structure of successful design, we are conscious of the most subtle kind of organization. When we contemplate nature, we are, likewise, struck by the delicately organized interdependence of all its elements. Nature is a network of ordered systems, the solar system, for example, just as civilization is a network of environments that we have created for ourselves.

When we study these humanly conceived environments, we find, as one might expect, that the more our organization resembles that of nature the more tolerable it is. In this respect, it is interesting to compare two photographs. The one on page 7 by Murray Greenberg, a New York City photographer, is of a grove of young saplings almost identical in appearance and, obviously, of identical physical structure. Despite the close similarities, they present a continuous landscape that is not in the least tedious, but full of variation and nuance. The above photograph is of *Habitat*, Montreal's prize-winning apartment complex. It is built of identical modules which, because of their aesthetic relationship to one another, do not present the repetitious and dreary aspect we associate with repeated architectural units. On the contrary, like that of the saplings, *it* is alive and exhilarating.

The art of early native cultures derives much of its energy from the direct use of natural materials. In this example of Tlingit art (right) we have a striking example of this. The artist has decided to allow the natural shapes of some parts of his necklace to determine the direction of his carving. He has left other parts entirely alone so that their intrinsic qualities can speak for themselves. The sculptural skill evident in this carving leaves no doubt that, in preserving much of the original character of the carefully selected materials, the artist *chose* to let his materials dominate the design. Parts of the carving were purposely allowed to appear untouched. Early art, from the woven masks of the South Pacific to the stone serpents of the ancient Mayans, is at its best when design accommodates itself to the material at hand. This maxim is no less true today. Yet, with the introduction of simulated materials and mass production, it is seldom discernible in the ''art'' and utilitarian objects of everyday life. In the classroom, however, there is no reason why such respect for the appreciation of materials cannot be as basic to good design as it once was.

The enthusiasm that native cultures felt for design and the sophistication and great expertise of their artists are exemplified in the elaborate Sisiutl mask from British Columbia pictured at the top of page 10. Designed for use in religious ceremonies, it is an indication of the significance of art to the people of this culture. Both it and the Tlingit necklace (right) tell us something else, that the peoples of all cultures from earliest times have created what we have come to know as *design* and have been moved by the aesthetic organization it implies.

Primitive cultures have also had to develop techniques and processes to put materials to use. Although many of these are understandably simple, all are ingenious and some surprisingly sophisticated and complex. The Benin bronze from Nigeria, page 11, is produced by a technique that requires the most delicate workmanship as well as an advanced knowledge of metallurgy and casting techniques. Likewise, the execution of the Polynesian tapa

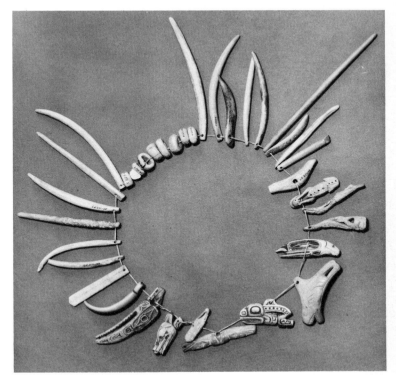

Courtesy of THE BROOKLYN MUSEUM.

9

Courtesy of THE BROOKLYN MUSEUM.

cloth on page 11 is dependent on much more than a passing acquaintance with the nature of fibers as well as extremely developed skills.

What is striking about these artifacts is the manner in which, in each case, the end result of the process concerned perfectly reflects the nature of the materials involved and so admirably accommodates the purposes it is intended for. The tapa cloth, for example, which might presumably be worn, draped or hung, would, with its checkerboard patterning, be as effective in any of these roles as it is flat, the way we see it here. The bronze, meant to be primarily monumental, not practical, is cast in low relief to catch the light. Hence the resultant shadows make the figures appear three-dimensional, even though they are not, and, therefore, more imposing.

When alien cultures encourage the native designer, as they have of late, to put his or her expertise to work for other than the original purposes or where other materials have been substituted for the traditional ones, the form often remains substantially the same. But because the chain of material and process is broken the vitality of the work is inevitably vitiated and its design significance destroyed.

There is an inherited urge in all of us to become involved in the design process even if today it consists of rearranging the furniture, organizing the garden, or reacting positively or negatively to the countless situations in which design plays a role. Tradition, closeness to nature, and the uncluttered life styles of primitive people made arriving at the rightness of design relatively uncomplicated. In contrast,

ourtesy of THE BROOKLYN MUSEUM.

the modern world is so crowded with objects and images and so devoid of tradition that our impulses are often short circuited and we become visually confused and inept. Consequently, our attitudes toward design need direction.

In the classroom, we have one of the few chances to turn the clock back. By working through the child's natural inclinations and by the introduction of stimulating materials and appropriate processes students are allowed to experience the excitement and satisfaction of working toward and achieving personally gratifying design goals.

Children need to be convinced that good design comes out of materials put to appropriate use. Because of the very obvious relationships between primitive processes and the materials which are associated with them, such processes make good models for student observation and for classroom practice. Some of the less complicated ways of working can be adapted directly for school use, primitive looms, for example. Youngsters are much more likely, too, to realize the relationships of material to design in objects produced by native artisans than in examples of present day design where complicated technology intervenes.

If there is a museum handy or good books, slides, or films available, it is worth the effort to acquaint students with primitive art to strengthen attitudes and supply inspiration.

DESIGN IN CONTEMPORARY ART

Nathan Lerner's *Eye in Window* (left) and Alexander Calder's untitled work on page 13 have a great deal in common. Almost certainly this similarity resides in the way our attention is drawn to the circular shape that dominates each composition. We can say that each artist in his own way has organized the elements which comprise his statement so that nothing detracts from the authority of the compelling motif in each. Yet Calder created his work strictly from imagination while Lerner used a camera to pluck his image from the environment.

No matter what the source of his visual material, it is the emphasis and placement an artist chooses to give each element in his work of art that decides what impact that element will have on the viewer. It is this visual order, the *design* of his artistic statement, that establishes an organizational structure that determines all other considerations. The artist may have gone through the process of arriving at this aesthetic order in the studio, in the darkroom, or in the environment, either spontaneously or in a much more studied manner. Whatever its nature or point of origin, the child goes through a similar process as he or she organizes two- and three-dimensional compositions in the classroom.

Children's art goes through as many stages as do children themselves. Their art, in fact, has proven to be a mirror of their social, mental, and creative growth. Quite understandably, their abilities and enthusiasms in art follow a sometimes predictable, sometimes erratic pattern, as does their overall development, particularly in preadolescence. We must remain alert to the dynamics of their changing attitudes toward both their own art and to art *per se* if art in the classroom is to be an effective element in their education.

The one constant that helps us link children's art at any one stage to art in general is the inherent urge within child and artist alike to establish a structure, a *design,* within which to organize the elements of his expression into some satisfying aesthetic order. This compulsion for order is also a definitive link between

Untitled, 1969, Alexander Calder, gouaché, 29½" X 41⅜". Collection, The Museum of Modern Art.

the earliest primitive art and the most avant garde of contemporary art. The analogy may at first seem exaggerated because of the extreme open-endedness of modern art. Yet, we must keep in mind that no matter how seemingly bizarre, spontaneous or even slapdash the approach of some of today's artists to their work, it is only that way because they want it that way.

This drive to establish order where none existed before attests to the fact that design is central to all forms of art and, as such, is significant to any art activity.

The teacher will take an important step in acquainting children with what constitutes a work of art by identifying the essential element of design present in the works by Calder and Lerner shown here, in ways children can empathize with and understand. Morever, design activities that emphasize aesthetic organiza-tion remain popular vehicles of expression even when preadolescents are embarrassed and disenchanted with their attempts at pic-ture making.

Art in the twentieth century is and has been in such a state of flux that our ideas of what constitute the fine arts have quite literally been turned topsy-turvy. Within the span of a single lifetime, such major movements as dada, cubism, surrealism, abstract expressionism and futurism have become the serious con-cern of artists, critics, and art historians alike. Add to these air art, pop art, op art, psychedelic art and kinetic art. The gamut of today's art media has been dramatically extended also by the rapid introduction of new techniques and new materals. For the first time artists are involved in areas of expression having to do with video, cinema, kinetics, the environment, laser beams, neon, polymers and acrylics. All this in an age when there are no restrictions and artists may create as they choose.

One must remember that all this freedom and opportunity for the artist follows hard on the heels of centuries of tradition and cautious change. Many of our fixations about what consitutes a work of art derive from past cultures, which decreed in completely arbitrary ways, what was artistically valid and what was not. The Renaissance is a particularly good example of this. Until recently the resulting misconceptions about values in art prevented primitive art and photography from being considered as possessing the aesthetic merit attributed to such traditional art areas as drawing and painting.

Today's teacher has the same freedom as today's artist. Instead of being confined as in the past to teaching skills associated with Renaissance ideas of what constitute "realism and beauty", teachers may gain inspiration from any of the current or established modes of expression and employ whatever contemporary or traditional media they feel are appropriate for effective classroom teaching.

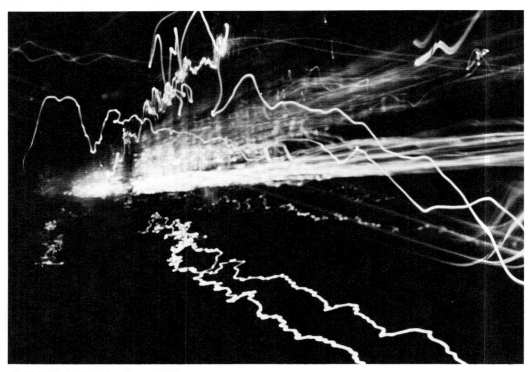

Car Light Study #3, Nathan Lerner, 1938

Because of its spontaneous origins within the individual, its unlimited range of expression and the openendedness of its activities, child art has much in common with contemporary art. When we consider design, there is even more evidence to convince us that recent developments in art provide good models for teaching design.

While design in the sense of aesthetic structure is a persistent element in all art, in contemporary pieces, such as the Calder on page 13 or Lerner's photograph *Car Light Study #3*, the organization of the work is often its principal component. As such, it immediately involves the viewer in the aesthetic structure around which the artist has designed his composition. In contrast, the design structure which provides the organization of a classic example of traditional art is not readily apparent to the viewer because attention is rivetted on the skilled rendering of the subject matter or caught up in the story line.

When we are working with children in design, contemporary art can have great significance for two reasons: it evokes lively discussion and interest as the child identifies such art with his own work, and from it the teacher can easily draw clear examples of whatever principles or approaches he or she wishes to emphasize.

An enthusiasm for modern art and a recognition of the common bonds between the child artist and the contemporary artist can heighten our appreciation of the highly personal and inventive aspects of children's art work. Modern art can bring us into contact with art ideas that suggest classroom activities appropriate to the enthusiasms of contemporary students. It can open up ways in which we can help them better understand and relate to the twentieth-century culture of which they are a part. It can suggest, too, a more reasoned attitude toward traditional skills as those associated with representational drawing, painting, and sculpture. In the classroom as in the contemporary art world such a tempered attitude will free students to express themselves through those means most compatible with their unique abilities and enthusiasms.

Man in Soft Hat Before a Wall, 1945, Jean Dubuffet, Lithograph, 14⁹/₁₆ x 9 ¹/₂. Collection, The Museum of Modern Art. Gift of Mr. & Mrs. Ralph F. Colin.

DESIGN AND THE PREADOLESCENT

The period of preadolescence is one of unevenness and ambiguity. Boys and girls from approximately nine to thirteen, with whom this book is particularly concerned, are full of zeal and energy, eager to learn, explore, and create. They are sensitive, affectionate, loyal, full of humor and much more aware than they ever were. Yet, while they are all these things, they can revert to the immature behavior of earlier years without warning. Often restless, irresponsible, touchy, and quixotic in their enthusiasms, they can be troublesome to instruct and difficult to reach.

Where once preadolescents were wholeheartedly poetic, imaginative and adventurous in their art, they are less fanciful, much more cautious, and often stiff and selfconscious. The easy symbolism and relaxed spatial organization of their early work no longer satisfy them as they make their first attempts at realism. Where once preadolescents drew and painted with abandon, now they are wary for fear that classmates will make fun of deeply expressed emotion or innovation.

To complicate matters, some students enter preadolescence later than others so that in the same class there may be a wide range of attitudes and abilities. Some students will typically approach drawing and painting in an emotional and impressionistic way while some

16

classmates will want to emphasize the factual and the visual. Such complications result in a classroom situation in which it is much more difficult for the teacher to fit instruction to the needs of the individual than it was in the lower grades. This is especially true if the class is large.

Preadolescence, too, is a time when children begin to make a sharp distinction between *drawing* and *design*. All too readily they will admit that so-and-so can draw well (and, therefore, is an artist) while they cannot. Preadolescence is a period when ideas too often run ahead of abilities so that disappointment and frustration are common. At this stage many children resort to cliches and copying to produce stodgy and derivative work if they haven't given up on picture making altogether.

Early art educators made the error of assuming that because older children were not as free and effective with crayons, paint, and clay as they once were that preadolescence was a period of creative latency. Now that the scope of art education has widened there is every evidence to the contrary. The eloquent and sensitive gestures of the nine-year-old pictured on page 16 indicate the amazing capacity for creative movement inherent in youngsters of this age. The exuberance of the young TV performer (right) is typical of the creative energy that the preadolescent releases in such activities as dramatics, video, and film making. Obviously, the problem in the middle school years is not that students lack creativity or enthusiasm for art but that our strategies for working with this challenging group are not always appropriate and, therefore, often prove ineffectual.

We must accept design as a basic component of art, as important to figurative work as to abstraction, as necessary to the crafts as to free form sculpture, not simply as a removed area having to do with patterning and decorative work. Only with this acceptance can we establish fresh approaches to preadolescent art. By using design we can cope effectively with the developmental obstacles that get in the way of some children, so that they can

benefit as fully from art activities as their energies and capabilities indicate they should.

Because design is fundamentally concerned with organization, the "content" of a design activity is not of primary concern. Content can be adapted to the needs of the individual, with, for instance, drawing skills emphasized or de-emphasized. When we reverse the procedure and make content the springboard for activity our approach cannot be as flexible. By emphasizing content we run the risk of losing the sincerity and eagerness of those children who have difficulty with representation.

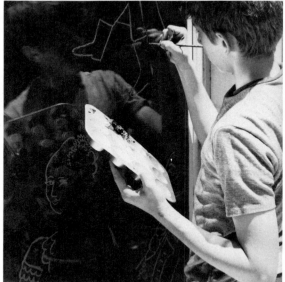

Children resort to other than creative ways of working when they have difficulty in their art work. For example, they may have trouble in arriving at ideas for picture or sculpture content, or they may be dissatisfied with their drawing, or confused by conventions concerning pictorial space (perspective, three-dimensional illusion), or may have difficulty painting up to a line or making a clay figure support itself. Design projects in which ideas grow out of materials and where aesthetic organization rather than representation is central to the activity do not involve children in such complications. Such projects free children to express themselves in ways that accomodate a broad spectrum of abilities and expectations. While experience indicates that most youngsters become more and more dissatisfied with their picture-making skills as they leave childhood behind, it is also apparent that they become increasingly sure of themselves in the physical and organizational skills necessary for success both in the crafts and in pure design. Consequently they become more satisfied with themselves and more enthusiastic about art when these areas are emphasized in the classroom.

The younger child is eager to communicate through art. The older student is eager to learn. And design activities are effective experiences through which to learn about art. A weaving technique, the steps of a printing process, a sculpture procedure, all are irresistible to the typical twelve-year-old who comes away from activities that feature such working methods with a feeling of having learned something. Having learned, he or she wants to put this knowledge to work. As the preadolescent becomes more and more secure in a new skill, he or she begins to experiment. In potato printing, to give only one example, this will almost certainly mean the discovery of a new excitement in color. What began as an enthusiasm to learn becomes a vehicle for successful expression.

It is when the students feel such success and so begin to relax and enjoy their art that confidence builds to the point where they are willing to try anything. They will possibly be

able to take occasional failure in stride. The effective teacher knows that it is important to build on success. This will be most frequent when the teacher works through activities that are closely allied to the abilities and dynamics of the age group involved.

Design activities, which, for the moment, may be characterized as those that children themselves designate as being opposite to activities incorporating visual representation, do not in themselves constitute a valid program in art education. Picture making, modeling, and the crafts are all just as essential to a well-rounded curriculum as is pure design. It is in design activities, however, that we find elements in the creative continuum of the child's development that remain virtually undisturbed during the unevenness of preadolescence. Design activities are valuable

agents in our efforts to keep the children's creativity alive so that they can function in all areas.

Some children are not as self-conscious about their representational work as are others. Confident in their abilities, they work as freely and effectively during preadolescence as they ever did, changing style and content to accomodate new interests and new emotions. They serve as reminders that some students will benefit from the structure and less subjective aspects of design much more than others. While all students gain from design experiences, there is much to be said for the type of classroom curriculum that is flexible enough to allow some students to concentrate much of their time in design-based activities while others are highly involved in picture making and sculpture.

PROCESS AND MATERIAL

Design cannot be seperated from the processes and materials which give it life. Whenever possible, design activities should not start with paper and pencil but with materials. Materials and processes can in themselves supply the most stimulating kind of motivation for design activity.

Both process and material must be carefully matched with the capabilities and interests of the age or ability of the group involved. Wire just right for an older class may be too difficult for a group of second graders; a printmaking technique easily understood by most ten-year-olds may be too complex for slow learners of the same age; setting up a certain type of loom may take so long that most elementary school youngsters will be bored with a proposed weaving project almost before it has begun. No matter how intrigued a teacher may be with a material or technique, if it does not sit well with the group it is intended for, it will never be effective in the classroom.

Even when all factors seem just right, children still need to be thoroughly acquainted with the intricacies of processes and materials if they are to work with them successfully. Once at ease with both process and medium, however, children are eager to begin work, secure in the knowledge that they will handle materials with understanding and work through the steps of a process with intelligence to create design forms that are personal, innovative, and worthwhile.

20

Introducing children to materials and processes is a demanding task. It is essential, however, that they be stimulated by the qualities unique to each material. Children must be convinced that best results are dependent on maximum use of these qualities. They should also understand the relationship between such qualities and the nature of the processes that make use of them. Lack of such understandings can only result in the child experiencing failure in even the most promising of activities. A clay figure that is oversupported by too much clay, for example, will be disappointing. It will look heavy and clumsy, unrelated to the original idea of the student. Similarly, a straw sculpture that does not capitalize on the lightness and strength of each straw will never become the airy, graceful, adventurous structure it could be. It is doomed to be ungainly and stolid.

Time is never better spent than in thoroughly exploring both material and process before beginning an activity. Involving the class itself in this introductory phase of each project is good strategy; having children "discover" the inherent qualities of a material or rationalize the steps of a technique on their own is even better. In some cases, however, failing a suitable response from the class, the teacher needs to supply important information, particularly if it is of a technical nature essential to the success of a process or technique.

Especially in the middle grades, some children tend to work intellectually, approaching a project involving real materials or based in the third dimension much as they would tackle a problem in drawing with pen and ink. They become stuck at the *idea* level rather than achieving the freedom of the *feeling* level. Others disregard the nature of the material or the process they are working with, concentrating, instead, on the portrayal of a personal or popular stereotype, a cartoon figure, perhaps, or the commercial symbol of some holiday. To combat such unproductive tendencies, it is doubly important that the child be enthused about the unique qualities of a process and excited about its materials so that these qual-

ities might be used to best advantage. This is another argument for making a clean break from pencil and paper and depending on the materials at hand as the design base for art activities.

THE TEACHER

The thesis that children are best able to express themselves through art when left free to work at a self-determined pace through ideas they have originated has a refreshing logic that is difficult to refute. It comes close to incorporating all the positive aspects of play into a teaching situation. Professionally, it suggests that the teacher's role is to set the stage, provide the materials and to intervene only when students need help to reach whatever goals they have set for themselves.

In actual fact, and especially with younger children when all factors are favorable, leaving children free to work independently is a productive and psychologically sound approach to classroom art. The effectiveness of such a teaching strategy is borne out by the many youngsters who work well this way both at home and in school. Indeed, such children find great satisfaction in working independently.

The teacher who must cope with a normal-sized class in an average classroom, particularly in the middle grades, soon realizes that such an unstructured approach has problems. There is a world of difference between teaching a class of 25 or 30 and teaching 25 or 30 individuals. Many preadolescent students are neither sufficiently resourceful nor self-motivated enough to carry on. Few classrooms are equipped for any kind of extensive diversification, and schools rarely have time slots conducive to self-initiated work.

In order to meet the goal of a truly creative experience for students the teacher must develop a structured approach to teaching that has two objectives: (1) it must give the teacher maximum control at the same time that (2) each child has maximum opportunity to work in his or her own way toward self-determined objectives.

The design activities presented in this book have been developed along lines that offer the teacher the chance to work with students as a class but which, at the same time, leave the children free to proceed toward highly personal goals that grow out of the materials being used. In each activity, it is the steps of the

process or technique that hold the class together and provide the focus of instruction. Either the material(s) or the method of working or both supplies the motivation and suggests any number of directions students can go with their self-conceived ideas.

With open-ended design activities, the teacher can play a more or less dominant role without interfering with individual creativity. For example, with one class, a good deal of time might be spent in the explanation of an activity, demonstrating each step in turn. With another, the best teaching strategy might be to stand back and allow students to establish their own ways of working.

There are advantages to children working on their own. There are also distinct benefits in the class working as one group or as several small groups. Preadolescents are beginning to interact with their peers in new social ways they have not shown an interest in previously

so that group undertakings, such as film making, mural making, and group sculpture projects, are popular and often very successful. Children at this age learn readily from one another and can be highly motivated merely by being associated with activities that involve the group. Success can be "contagious" in the middle grades. The drama and excitement of a first print being pulled or the first batik coming out of the dye can be extremely stimulating. Students who have not as yet finished their projects will work with renewed enthusiasm after having seen what their classmates have accomplished.

The effective teacher always allows students as much freedom as possible both to initiate and to work through design activities on their own. But the teacher must calculate the approach to use with each class and each individual in order to maximize the satisfaction and success that each child can experience.

THE CLASSROOM

Children are sensitive to the environment in which they work. In order to provide a stimulating environment the room in which design activities take place should be attractive and cheerful, having display areas where exhibitions change frequently. If it is well organized with appropriate and accessible tools, materials, and work areas it will enable the student to work efficiently without frustration and make it more possible for the teacher to teach effectively.

If a special room is available for art instruction it would be a good idea if it resembled an artist's studio. The discipline that art presupposes and that of an academic area are worlds apart for both practical and philosophic reasons. It is logical to conclude that the environment that accomodates art education should reflect that difference. Design activities, in such a case, are best served by good light, large moveable tables, plenty of storage space, big display areas and as much sink space as possible.

A specific art area is desirable, but in all probability the average classroom teacher will have to carry on both art and design activities without such amenities. However, there are advantages to having the classroom teacher teach design in his or her own room. Classroom teachers above anyone else, have an intimate knowledge of their students' enthusiasms, skills, and attitudes and can more easily integrate art and design with other subjects.

The classroom teacher knows when it is important to allot additional instructional time to an individual or a small group and can arrange to do so if most subjects are taught in one classroom. If equipment is limited in such areas as print or film making the teacher can allow small groups to work with such equipment in turn throughout the day while other students are doing academic work. However, in all these circumstances, the teacher must be flexible enough in classroom organization so that such positive arrangements will work to advantage.

The author's experience as a classroom teacher indicates that incorporating ongoing art and design experiences into the school day

has many other benefits. Art and design experiences are effective in absorbing the energies of those students who tend to complete academic assignments ahead of their classmates. They help children internalize concepts through such long-term projects as films, murals, and puppet productions. They provide enough time for children who feel inadequate in other areas to build up self-confidence. And, finally, they realize maximum use of equipment and make the classroom a generally livelier and more inviting environment for learning.

Certainly practicality must proceed creativity when art activities take place in the classroom. There should be a specific location for each piece of equipment. Scrap materials should be sorted and stored in labelled containers. There should be storage and drying areas for completed work and work in progress. Set routines need to be organized to facilitate handing out supplies and cleaning up.

Design activities lend themselves to the kind of controlled organization necessary for suc-cessful teaching with normal or over-sized classes in an ordinary classroom situation. Each project described in the book suggests a basic procedure that is not difficult to handle under such circumstances. Additional suggestions are given for expanding the concept involved and for freeing up procedures when conditions permit. In slide making, for example, ways of working with dry materials are recommended as an initial approach with the introduction of wet materials proposed as an elaboration of the original idea.

Projects incorporating concepts and goals which might be confusing to children have been avoided along with activities that require elaborate equipment. Step-by-step procedures constructed with a respect for the child's creativity are demonstrated. Each procedure is calculated to provide opportunities for the teacher to ensure that the student both understands what is expected and is at ease with what he or she is doing. It is hoped that teachers finding these procedures effective will be encouraged to formulate other design strategies along similar lines.

EXPERIMENTATION

Whatever the nature of a design activity may be, experimentation with its materials should be a built-in component of the experience. Playing with a material is probably the best way to find out about it. Some activities encourage experimentation more than others; splattering or dripping wet paint on to wet paper or, in slide making, floating inks in oil are two that would seem to begin and end with experimentation.

Others, such as activities to do with cut paper or other dry materials, involve manipulation of shapes in two-dimensional space rather than tranformations of the material itself. Straw sculpture, for example, involves architectural manipulation in three-dimensional space but the straws themselves remain unchanged.

No matter what the nature of experimentation, it is the prelude to any kind of creative work in design. The teacher plays an important role in this first phase of a design project by encouraging exploration of materials and processes, by providing a wide enough spectrum of supplementary materials so that experimentation can be expansive and rewarding, and by demonstrating the potential of new materials with which the class is totally unfamiliar.

Processes, as much as materials, lend themselves to experimentation and should be introduced in such a way that the student feels at liberty to explore further possibilities once the central skill has been mastered.

Experimentation for its own sake, however, eventually becomes tedious and counter-productive. At some point, there should be an easy transition, appropriate to the activity, from the testing period to the actual design operation. In slide making, for example, it is worthwhile to have a projector handy which a student can use to project the same slide over and over again until a satisfying visual effect is achieved. In composing a collage, the same student may work differently, moving material around until a satisfactory composition is developed and then gluing all its parts down at one time with no further manipulation.

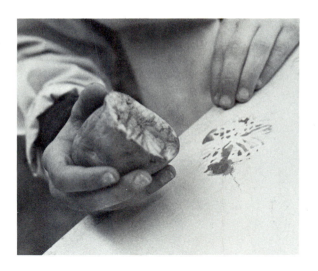

While the art educator sees in process the most valid aspect of an art activity and while the student can be completely involved and enthusiastic when working, it is the end product that is always of most importance to the preadolescent. To underestimate the significance of the child's assessment of successful achievment would be naive; yet, to overlook the value of process would be equally so. The trick is to convince the child that the worth of the finished work is inextricably connected with the process that produced it.

Children are quick to place a premium on whatever is produced in class. If excellence in drawing is the criterion of quality (in the student's mind) and the child is convinced his or her completed drawing is childish whatever the excellence of what is accomplished, the effort will be considered a waste of time. On the other hand, if the evaluation of a project hinges on a more intangible value judgement to do with, say, inventiveness, and there is a wide assortment of ways to bring the activity to a successful conclusion, students are more likely to be pleased with their efforts. It goes without saying that the more successful chil-

dren feel in their work, the more enthusiastic they will become. And, the more at ease and effective they will be in future undertakings.

This being the case, constant attention needs to be directed toward convincing students that their work is indeed worthwhile. Class discussions at the conclusion of a project, exhibitions of work in which everyone is included, avoidance of any kind of punitive marking, all contribute to a feeling of well-being and a sense of accomplishment.

As creative activity in the classroom is fairly predictable, it is not difficult to presuppose the order into which the child's experiences will fall in a design project.

To begin with, children acquaint themselves with the nature of the materials and processes appropriate to the activity at hand and explore their possibilities. This might take some time or just a few minutes. Next, motivated by the results of these explorations, they see design possibilities in the relationship of one material to another or a construction arrangement that seems to work well or, perhaps, a combination of shapes in which they sense the beginnings of a composition. They may even conjure up an image that would make an effective theme for a print, a collage, or a sculptural piece. Whatever the circumstance, they eventually arrive at an idea which not only triggers immediate action but determines how they will expend their energies to achieve their design goals.

Without this idea the creative process is short-circuited and youngsters become either immobile or derivitive, copying what other students are doing. They may even resort to some hackneyed theme inappropriate to the process or the material involved.

It is at this point in the development of children's designs that the teacher plays a most important role both in directing students toward action-generating ideas that are conducive to creative work and in organizing classroom situations that are stimulating enough so that such ideas are not hard to come by. The activities outlined in this book are meant to be of assistance in this regard.

FROM PROCESS TO RESOLUTION

Once students have arrived at ideas that give direction to their projects, they are well on the way to the satisfactory solution of the design problems they have set for themselves. In some cases, the ensuing *process* may take only a few minutes, as in the case of slide making. In contrast, several classroom sessions might be required to complete a cardboard print. Neither situation is foolproof, however. Because the technique of slide making is not demanding, the results could be superficial; because of the steps involved in printmaking, the finished product could well be mechanical and stiff and not reflect the fresh and innovative statement the student had meant to convey.

The point that is worth considering is that, even when students are heading toward some sort of resolution of their original ideas, no step of the process in each instance should be considered inevitable. This is where design ideas that grow from techniques or materials rather than "true-to-life" themes have an advantage. Obviously, as they are not imagined in anything but general terms, the direction in which a student is working can remain flexible at all times.

The teacher, of course, can be instrumental in assuring the creative resolution of each project; keeping hands off in one case yet providing considerable support in another. For example, suggesting that a more *complex* approach might *enrich* a slide while, conversely, helping a student to see that *simplifying* a print could *strengthen* its design. In all cases, however, the teacher's role does not include advocating any particular end product.

The more secure children feel in an art activity, the stronger and more personal will be their expression. Closely structured design projects such as this one, that let youngsters make all the artistic decisions, give them confidence in their art abilities and prepare them to participate fully and effectively in progressively freer and more complicated activities.

The teacher in the procedure outlined here begins by giving very specific directions in a step-by-step manner *but* takes pains to see that personal decisions as to where to place a line or what color to use are left up to each individual. By the latter part of the activity, the initial controls are completely relaxed and the students are free to create their own personally conceived designs.

1. *Cutting out two or three areas from a design and then mounting it on colored or black construction paper so that the background shows through creates a novel and interesting effect.*
2. *When straight-line designs are displayed as a mural with one design touching the next there is enough similarity in each design to make the over-all effect both organized and dramatic.*

1.

2.

31

1.

2.

3.

1. *Following a step-by-step procedure, two straight lines are drawn, either by ruler or freehand, from the top of the paper to the bottom. Black crayon gives a sharp, reassuring line.*

2. *At the direction of the teacher, the paper is turned sideways. Three straight lines are drawn from one side to the other breaking up the paper into more and smaller areas.*

3. *Additional straight lines are drawn. These may be placed anywhere as long as they form closed areas which are the least complicated to color.*

4. *A personally selected color scheme is chosen. Crayons are used firmly to fill in the design areas.*

5. *Crayons of the chosen colors are applied to fill all the spaces. White is used where color is thought not to be appropriate. The original lines are gone over in black to accentuate the linear quality of the composition.*

6. *The completed design stands out boldly against its black construction paper mount.*

4.

5.

6.

Elementary school children like to build things — tree houses, snow forts, sand castles. They like to build directly with the materials they have on hand. Such building acitivities, like many other aspects of childhood play, contribute directly to the art education of the child.

Constructing in materials without first planning on paper helps to develop a strong design sense. Elementary school art programs can provide many opportunities for youngsters to construct and design in actual materials. Projects emphasizing design through construction are easily taught in the classroom. The child should be frequently challenged to literally *build* designs with materials suitable for his or her age group. In such projects the material should be allowed to dictate the form the design will take, instead of being forced to conform to some pattern or plan drawn up beforehand.

In this project the problem is to build a design from a number of ordinary drinking straws (the least expensive, non-plastic straws are best), using only straws, a few small pins, some quick-drying cement and a pair of scissors.

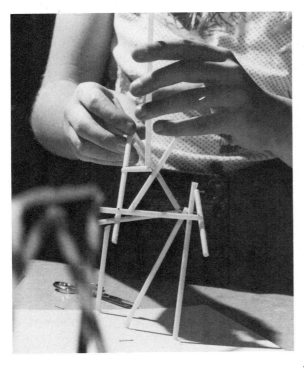

Building a Straw Design

1. *Building a straw design is an architectural undertaking. The design should look good and stand upright, too. So, first, experiment with a few straws. Try to find the means to construct a base that will be sturdy but, at the same time, graceful.*

2. *Once a plan for a base has been worked out, the parts are cemented together with quick-drying glue.*

3. *Straws may be cut to any size and glued directly to other straws or cut at an angle to fit more snugly. Pins can be used also to hold parts together until the glue dries, then pulled out.*

4. *Other pins can be pushed through certain straws to make permanent supports . . . . . .*

5. *. . . . . . for other straws . . . . .*

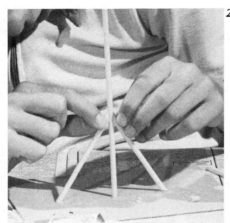

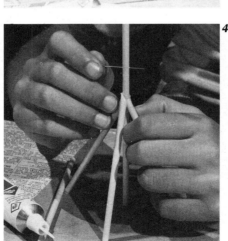

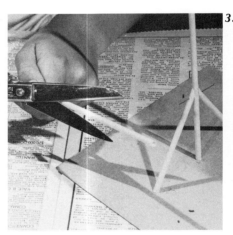

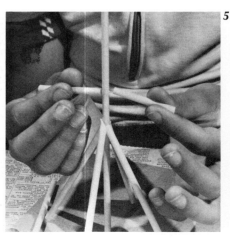

6. . . . . . . which are glued in place but rest on the support pins. Pinning and gluing some of the straws in the construction in this manner will make it extremely sturdy so that elements can be "cantilevered" out from the central section, to bring excitement and a sense of daring to the completed sculpture.

7. Once the basic parts of a design are in place one can experiment with different arrangements of straws until an appealing sculptural design is found. In this photograph a pin is put in at a slant as the straw that fits on to it is meant to lean out at an angle.

8. Inspect the project from all sides to see if it has achieved a design quality that is aesthetically satisfying. If it is, the sculpture is finished. All that remains to do is to check its construction to see that all parts are firmly glued in place and unnecessary pins removed.

6.

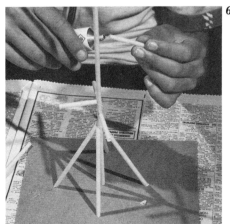

7.

8.

STRAIGHT LINE SCULPTURE

There are many inexpensive classroom sculpture materials that have the same rigid, linear qualities characteristic of drinking straws. Obviously, sculptural designs constructed of these materials share the familiar straight line appearance of straw sculpture. In fact, they are built in much the same way, one element cemented to the next with quick-drying glue. When a material such as balsa wood is yielding enough, straight pins can be used, as in straw sculpture, to speed up construction and make each finished project sturdier.

While all these materials share the same basic characteristics, each one is different in its own way. While balsa wood strips are extremely light, cardboard tubes are comparatively heavy. Toothpicks come only in short lengths. Drinking straws are hollow. Spaghetti is too tough for pins when dry but, if soaked in warm water, becomes so soft and pliable that it may be twisted into an unending variety of non-linear shapes. Whatever the special property of a material, it should dictate the nature of the design sculpture that grows from it. Particularly in the classroom, respecting the uniqueness of a material makes for bolder sculptural statements and fewer problems with construction.

Some common materials, other than drinking straws, that lend themselves to straight-line sculpture are: natural straws, balsa wood strips, fine spaghetti or spaghettini, cardboard tubes, dowels, toothpicks, stiff cardboard strips, dried reeds, ice cream and popsicle sticks, tongue depressors, tightly rolled paper tubes.

Indiscriminate decoration can detract from the vitality and clean cut economy of a straight line sculpture. Additions of colored paper or tissue, buckram or tinted acetate applied in the geometric mode of this kind of construction can accentuate its line quality and so enhance its effect. Both poster paint and spray paint, applied in an over-all manner, can often be the unifying element that pulls a linear composition together. More often than not, however, the untouched materials themselves are as attractive as any decoration.

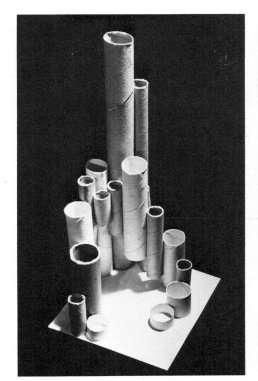

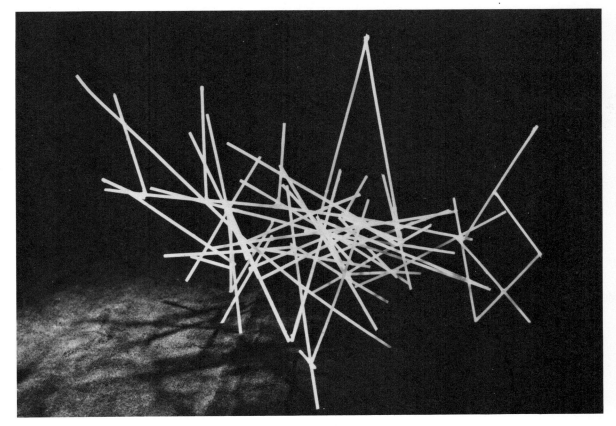

WIRE SCULPTURE

Working in the third dimension has a special appeal for elementary school children. They enjoy handling tangible materials and manipulating them into sculptural forms. Wire is especially appealing to them because it is yielding enough to allow the most intricate shapes to be coaxed from it; yet, resistant enough to give it a challenging, physical quality.

In terms of an art element, wire is pure line. It has none of the mass of clay or the surface texture of wood or fabric. No matter what content or form the child or artist has in mind, with wire, it must be translated in terms of line.

Many artists have delighted in the crisp, economical statements that can be made with wire. Alexander Calder, for instance, used wire as the basic material for his well-known *Circus*. Although it is a sculptural medium, there is a strong resemblance in the line quality of a wire sculpture to the sharp, snappy feeling of a line drawing in pencil or pen and ink. In

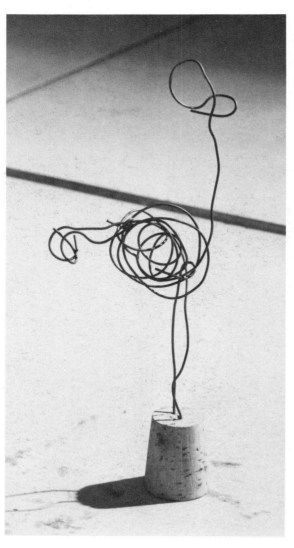

fact, children can *sketch* with wire, bending it this way or that. Then if the effect is not completely gratifying, they can bend it again in a different way to achieve a more satisfying shape.

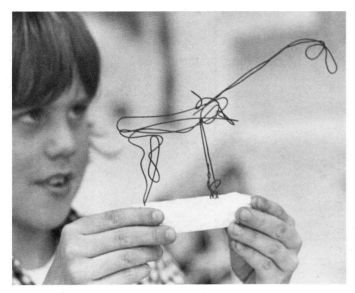
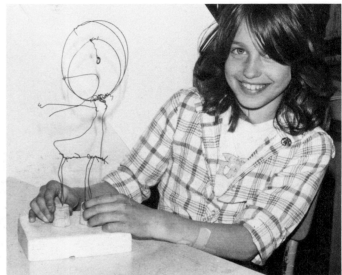

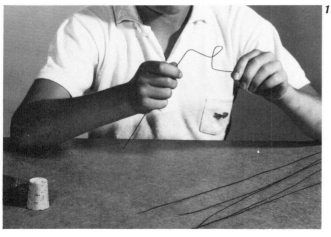

1.

1. To design a piece of wire sculpture, experiment by bending a piece of soft wire into some interesting shapes.
2. As soon as a design idea is decided upon begin to shape the first element of the composition.
3. Soft wires, such as copper wire and florists' wire, are so malleable that one can easily bend them around a finger to achieve certain effects.
4. A thermos cork, a block of soft wood, or a square of Styrofoam all make good bases for wire sculpture. In some cases, one may have to start a hole in the material into which one "leg" of the design then can be inserted.
5. In this case, when all three parts of the sculpture were complete, they were fitted into a cork base.

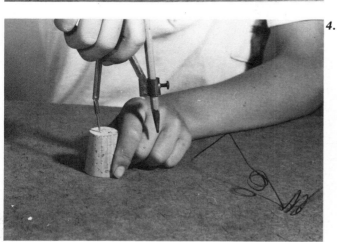

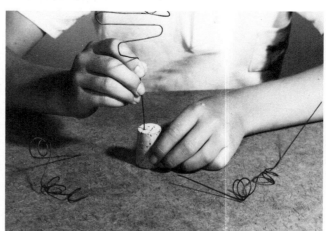

6. Next, the various elements of the design were arranged to assume a pleasing relationship.

7. At this point, it is wise to study the sculpture from all sides, adjusting an ''arm'' here, adding a loop there until each element of the design seems in harmony with every other part.

8. Only when the final adjustment is made to the complete satisfaction of the sculptor is the design finished.

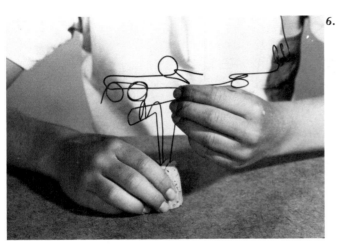

6.

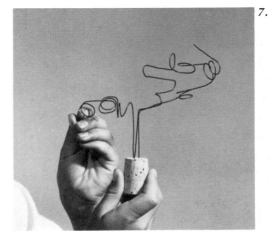

7.

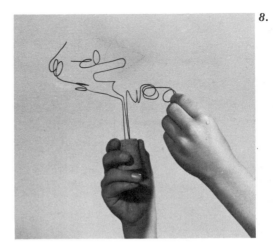

8.

Florists' wire, which is used here, is an excellent sculptural medium. It is soft enough for children to control, yet sufficiently resistant to make it fun to work with. It is strong enough to support quite extended designs and stiff enough to retain even the most complex shapes. Not expensive, it can be obtained in a variety of useful lengths and weights from any dealer in florists' supplies. Children can use copper wire, galvanized wire, and even stove pipe wire, each in a light weight gauge, for wire sculpture. Most hardware stores carry these kinds of wire. Wire sculpture can stand alone, can be hung, or can be supported by bases of soft wood, plaster, foam, or cork.

FROM LINE TO DESIGN WITH TEMPERA

Even the simplest of elementary school painting projects can be more difficult for some children than we realize. Few youngsters in the upper elementary grades, for example, approach picture making with the same easy abandon they did in the primary grades. Often, an empty sheet of manila paper can take on frightening proportions for children whom inspiration has passed by.

There are many ways, of course, to help hesitant children realize their painting potential. Most methods, unfortunately, begin to lose their effectiveness as the group approaches average classroom size. The activity suggested here, luckily, can be used as successfully with large groups as with small.

In this project students first break up the surface of their papers into a number of design areas. They do this by using a brush to draw one or several continuous lines that loop back and forth over themselves. The individual determines the character of the line in the painting. If a smooth, flowing line is used, a series of lazy elliptic areas is created. If a severe, spiky line is drawn, the shapes will be angular and geometric. On dry paper a line will be sharp and distinct. On wet paper it will be diffuse and subtle. Although each member of the class begins a painting with a continuous line, each

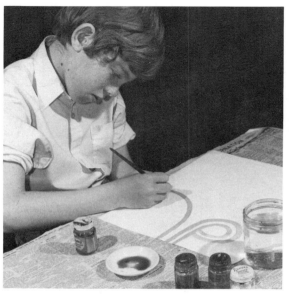

46

composition, even at this initial stage, can be highly personal.

Once the basic lines are established, students can begin to work with color and texture in each area that has been created. Secure with a structure on which to "hang" a design, children now feel confident and ready to build their compositions each in a personal way. At this point, the original line can remain a dominant force or it can be allowed to show only now and again. It can also be completely obliterated as new forms occur to the young painter.

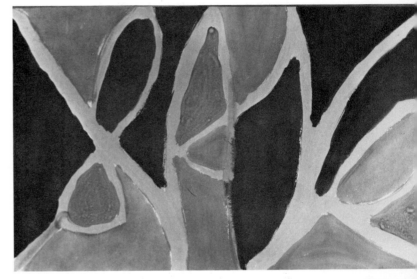

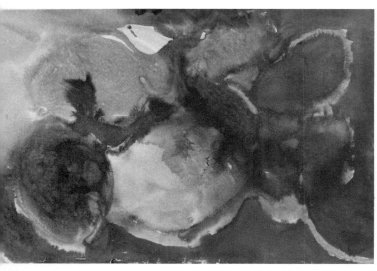

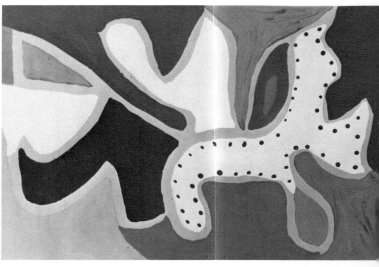

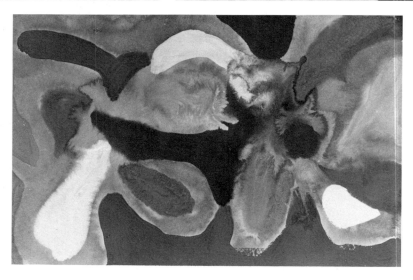

1.

2.

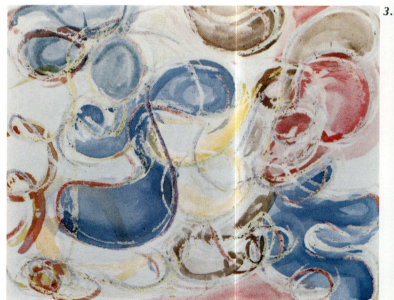

3.

1. Wet tempera into wet paper.
2. Burlap, toothpicks, styrofoam, string, fibers to form collage with tempera paint added.
3. Wax crayons tied in a bundle and run at random over the surface of the paper. Water color painted freely into the areas created.

4. String glued to cardboard to establish design forms. Tempera paint added.

5. Freehand drawing in black board chalk. Tempera paint up to and over chalk.

6. Blackboard chalk outline. Tempera paint up to chalk but not over it. Original chalk line still visible as part of the composition.

POTATO PRINTING

Printing has long been a popular classroom activity. The opportunities for creative invention which this technique offers never fail to inspire youngsters to produce new designs and refreshingly spontaneous prints.

Potato printing is a primitive method of printmaking and does not lend itself to complicated subject matter. A non-objective approach making use of natural shapes as well as utilizing the blemishes on the cut surface of the potato will always produce a more effective print than one evolved by a slicker, more sophisticated treatment. Because of its primitive quality and limited size a potato print does not show to advantage as an isloted design. It is more effective when repeated in an "all over" pattern with each motif printed close to the next.

Before printing, each potato (old ones are best) must be washed. It is then cut in half by the teacher with a large-bladed kitchen knife

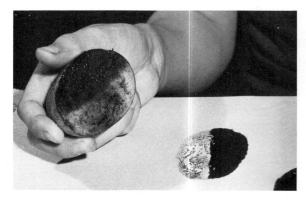

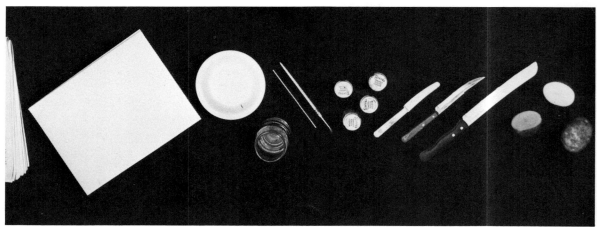

52

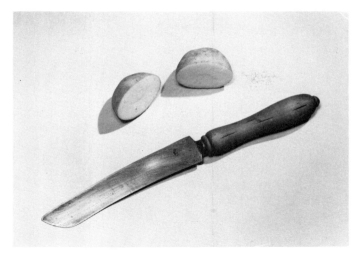

(top left). This will ensure a sustained straight cut across the potato, thus, avoiding a warped surface. Potatoes should be placed cut side down on newspaper or newsprint until needed. The paper will absorb any excess moisture that could interfere with printing.

When children are ready to attempt more advanced printmaking processes requiring the use of knives, they should use either serrated paring knives or serrated plastic picnic knives to carve their designs. The serrations make it difficult for them to cut themselves (top right).

Before beginning actual printmaking, children should be given every opportunity to become familiar with the technique of potato printing. Tempera paint is brushed sparingly on the uncarved cut surface of the potato. A sheet of newsprint or construction paper is placed on top of a springy pad of newspaper pages. The painted cut potato is pressed firmly against the surface of the paper and rocked gently back to front and from side to side (bottom photos). This ensures a crisp, even impression.

A good print should use so little paint that it dries almost immediately. Its shape should be clearly defined and the texture of the potato's cut surface clearly visible. Each print should achieve approximately the same intensity and color value as the next although slight variations in print quality and color are almost impossible to avoid.

Potato Printing with Painted Designs

1. *Designs can be painted in tempera directly on the cut surface of the potato. A little experimentation will indicate how thick the paint should be for the paper used. The thinner the paint, however, the less brilliant the printed color. The design may be simple or complicated but lines too close to one another tend to run together when printed.*

2. *When the design is complete, the painted surface is pressed against the paper and the potato rocked back and forth to ensure a well-defined image.*

1.

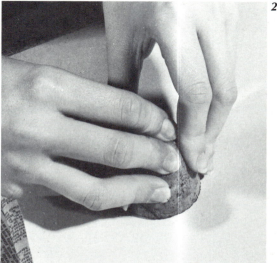

2.

3. Although the act of printing uses up most of the paint, there is still enough left on the potato so that the design is clearly visible. This leftover paint can be used as a guide if the design is to be repeated or can be printed off on scrap paper if a new design is to be painted on.

4. For more accurate "registration" in printing an over-all pattern, the surface of the potato can be partially cut away to leave a square or a rectangle, triangle and so on. The design is then painted on this raised area.

5. Notice how the perimeters of the design area are clearly visible.

6. The results are identical to those of the first procedure but the printmaker has more control over the placement of the design.

3.

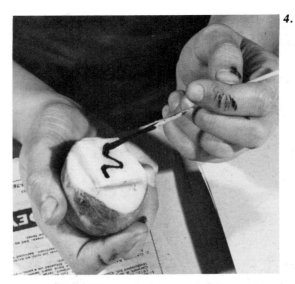

4.

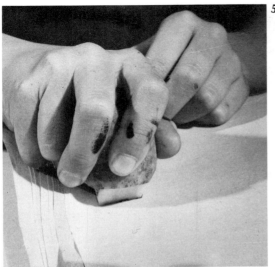

5.

6.

Potato Printing with Sgraffito Designs

A traditional way of decorating pottery is to coat the clay piece with slip (colored clay mixed with water) and then to scratch design forms through the slip to reveal the clay underneath. Potters refer to this scratching-away process as "sgraffito."

A similar method can be applied to potato printing to produce design prints that have a characteristic "scratched-away" quality. The prints on the left were produced by the "sgraffito" method of potato printing.

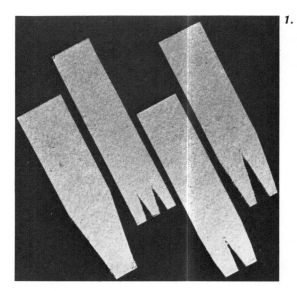

1.

2.

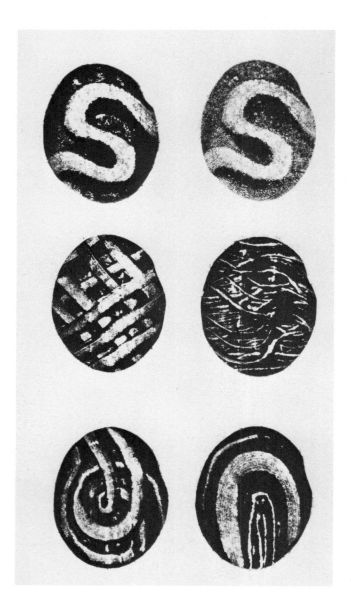

1. *Although paper clips, pencil points, bits of sponge and the like can be used to produce "sgraffito" effects in potato printing, cutout cardboard scrapers, such as these, are extremely effective.*
2. *The first step in the "sgraffito" process is to coat the cut surface of the potato with a thin layer of tempera paint.*
3. *The scraper is pulled through the wet paint to leave a "design trail."*
4. *The potato is printed. Where the paint has been scraped away the color of the paper shows through to define the design shape.*

Potato Printing with a Stencilled Design

The use of stencils in potato printing produces the opposite effect of that obtained by the sgraffito method.

In this row of stencilled potato prints note how the design area is always more defined than the background. Observe how the design element holds up even though there are large variations of tonal quality between one print and the next.

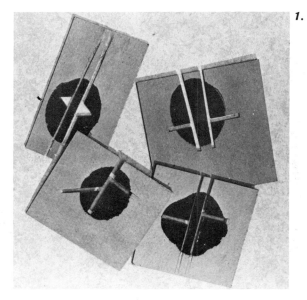

1. Stencils are cut from small pieces of scrap cardboard. Simple straight-line motifs are best.

2. The cut potato is given a thin coat of tempera paint and pressed down on the cardboard.

3. The potato is then printed on paper in the usual manner.

4. The stencil has absorbed most of the paint from those parts of the potato which came in contact with the cardboard but has left actual design areas at full strength. A stencil print is always an effective combination of a well-defined design motif standing out sharply against a subdued and textured background.

Carved Potato Prints

The traditional method of potato printing consists of cutting away some parts of the surface of the potato so that what remains is a raised and printable design area. However, children need some guidance if they are to be successful in using this approach. They need to be directed toward natural ways of working that are best suited to this kind of printmaking. For example, simple designs based in straight-line cuts (illustrations, page 60) are much more likely to print well than those involving elaborate curves and realistic forms. When carving designs in this way it is best to use the knife at an angle to make *V*-shaped cuts that give maximum support to the printing surface.

Overprinting is a way of elaborating on a design theme without introducing complex cutting procedures. We see this technique demonstrated in photos 4 and 5 (page 62). First an overall pattern consisting of repeated prints of the uncarved potato is completed. Then a straight-line design is carved into the same potato and printed over the initial prints in a different color. This could be repeated several times with the carved design becoming progressively more skeletal as more and more cuts are made.

The "Z" motif below is the basic element of the over-all pattern to the right. You can see how the original print is strengthened by overprinting with more white and changed by overprinting with blue, in one case, and orange, in the other.

1. *The two surfaces of the halves of a potato are carved away to leave raised design areas.*
2. *The design areas are painted different colors (all of which can be printed at the same time) and printed in rows by eye to create an over-all pattern. See illustration at right.*

1.

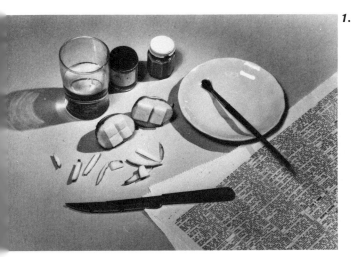

2.

61

3.

3. A melon baller is used here to carve a design. Because it has a circular blade it is as easy to cut a circle with it as it is to cut a straight line with a conventional paring knife.
4. The shape of the potato plus the circular cut combine to make an effective design motif.
5. Circular cuts are made in both surfaces of a halved potato and the edges are cut away to make a square of one half.
6. This provides the design elements for an over-printed pattern.

4.

5

6

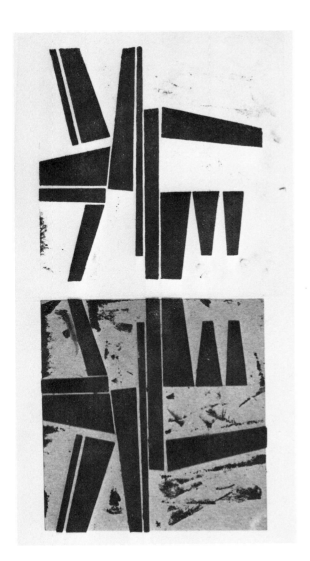

Printmaking in the elementary school is one of the most satisfying of art activities, but it does not have to be an expensive one. Some of the most exciting techniques require only the cheapest of materials. Demonstrated here is a method by which elementary school children can produce sharp and consistent prints using only scrap cardboard as a printing base.

While only the simplest means have been used to produce the prints shown here, they have many of the characteristics and qualities of those produced by more complicated processes. The very primitiveness of the medium can often direct children to produce tremendously vigorous prints which, somehow, do not seem easily achieved with more expensive materials. Nevertheless, limitations to such a basic technique exist. They must be realized and the class encouraged to use forthright design forms.

The method described here can be varied by using more than one kind of cardboard to form the printing surface, or by adding areas of sponge or coarse sandpaper to give texture to designs. Different colors of printing ink and a variety of papers will help extend the possibilities of this inexpensive but exciting technique.

When glue is used to adhere the parts of a cardboard print design to the base, only one coat is needed. Lengths of scrap cardboard make handy gluing tools when used as demonstrated in the photo on the immediate right.

When rubber cement is the adhesive, a coat should be applied to both the base and the part to be attached to it. The cement should be allowed to dry and the cemented part pressed on to the base.

1. A good first activity in cardboard printing involves precut cardboard shapes. In such an activity, random shapes should be cut from scrap cardboard on the paper cutter in advance of the printing session. The student then arranges and rearranges a selection of these shapes until a pleasing design is developed.
2. Parts of the design are then glued to a cardboard base.
3. When the complete design is glued into place, any stray ends are cut to match the edges of the base.
4. A three-quarter inch length of water-based printers' ink is squeezed onto an inking slab. The slab here is glass, but it could just as well be a sheet of plexiglas, a cookie tray, or even a formica table top.
5. A brayer is used to roll the ink back and forth until its roller is covered with a thin, even layer of ink.
6. Using the inked brayer, the student transfers the ink to the design.

1.

2.

After everything is cemented into position and the glue is dry, varnishing both the design and its cardboard base is a worthwhile procedure. Althought it means that students cannot print the same day they complete their designs, the wait is good insurance against the cardboard pulling apart and causing disappointments.

Students need to be reminded that their designs will print in reverse. At the elementary level, children will probably not be too upset when they find they are printing mirror images of their abstract designs. But, when content or lettering is involved, reverse prints can be frustrating.

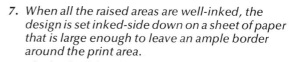

7. When all the raised areas are well-inked, the design is set inked-side down on a sheet of paper that is large enough to leave an ample border around the print area.

8. The back of the printing base is rubbed so that the ink will be pressed into the paper.

9. Both the inked design and the paper are turned over so the paper is now on top. The paper is rubbed with the fingertips (or a clean brayer or the bowl of a spoon) until there is no point at which the inked design is not in close contact with the paper. Here, as the paper is thin, you can actually see how the ink has transferred from the cardboard to the paper.

10. Finally, the paper is pulled back gently to reveal the print.

Shirt cardboard is excellent for printmaking. A sheet cut in half provides just enough material for both the base and the design components of a printing *block* (the glued design ready for printing). For example, one shirt cardboard yields just enough material for the project described above.

Double-sided corrugated cardboard also make a novel printmaking material. Only one sheet is needed and no gluing is required. With a razor blade or sharp pocket knife, cut closed design shapes through the layer of paper glued to the top edges of the corrugations. Peel off the paper within these areas to reveal the corrugations underneath. Then, ink up and print.

66

1. A slightly more complex way of arriving at a design composition than that described on pages 64, 65 and 66 involves drawing. Two pieces of cardboard and a sheet of paper are cut to the same size. A design is drawn on the paper with the shapes kept fairly simple so the student will not run into trouble cutting them out of the cardboard.

2. The design is traced on both pieces of cardboard.

3. The design is cut from one piece.

4. Each design piece is pasted into position on the base. Now printing can proceed in the manner described on pages 64 and 66.

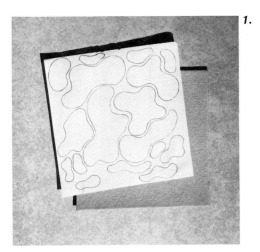

1.

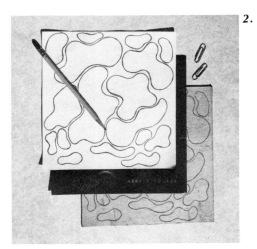

2.

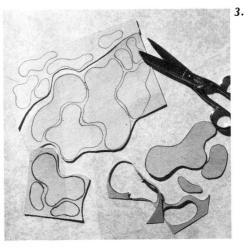

3.

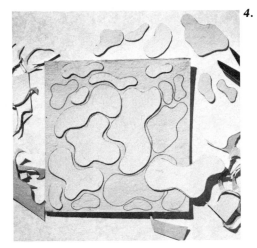

4.

68

Cardboard Printing in Color

The richness of classroom color prints suggest they are the product of a complicated technique but, in fact, the reverse is true. Very beautiful prints can be achieved by simple, straightforward means. For instance, to overprint in color:

1. Four or five prints (to experiment with) should be produced in a basic color using the technique described on pages 64, 66. White on black is a good combination, but any color that is not too dark will do. Printing on colored construction paper will automatically add another color.

2. Without re-inking, the cardboard is printed on newspaper until it is clear of the original color.

3. Using a clean inking slab and a clean brayer, a new color is rolled onto the brayer.

4. The cardboard design is re-inked and lowered onto one of the prints. The top edge of the cardboard design should match the top edge of the printed design. The other prints may be overprinted later.

5. The cardboard design is pressed against the paper so that the ink adheres. The paper and the cardboard are turned over. The paper (now on top) is rubbed with the fingertips or the curve of a spoon.

6. The paper is peeled gently from the cardboard to reveal a two-color print. The same procedure is followed for each additional color.

Variations on this technique will add delightful nuances to the results of all-over printing. Spots of color may be added to the cardboard design with a fingertip, a pencil point, a bit of sponge. The brayer may be only partially inked or inked with spots or bands of color. Wet ink on wet ink will give a different effect than wet on dry. Removing ink from the cardboard design with the end of a paint brush or scraping it off in some areas with a knife blade will create another kind of print surface. "Off-registering" a color will give a three-dimensional feeling.

1. *A third approach to evolving a cardboard print design is to cut two pieces of cardboard and a sheet of black construction paper to the same size. Cut out some design elements from the construction paper.*
2. *Place the cutout construction paper shapes at random on one of the cardboard sheets and trace around them.*
3. *Cut out the shapes.*
4. *Assemble the cardboard shapes into a composition on the second sheet of cardboard. Glue them in place. Print, using the method described on pages 64, 65 and 66.*

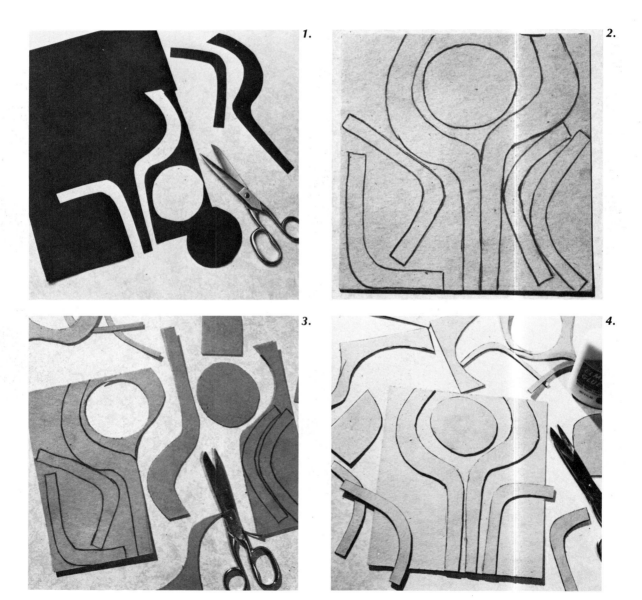

1. The most efficient way to organize for printmaking in the classroom is to set up a printing station or printing stations (if there is enough equipment). Here is a typical station; the table is covered with newspaper taped down so it will not shift, a clean inking slab and brayer are to the right of the design and the design is positioned on top of an open magazine which sits with its cover hanging over the edge of the table.

2. Now the inking has begun. The ink is rolled out in a thin layer. The brayer has made some "passes" across the design. The printmaker had been careful to ink the edges of his design so some ink has smudged the magazine page.

3. The design is fully inked. You can't see it but the inky magazine page has been turned and hangs over the edge of the table with its ink spots sandwiched between itself and the magazine cover. Paper covers the design and a clean brayer (it could be a spoon) is handy for pressing the paper against the ink.

4. The paper is pulled back to show that the edges of the print are clean because the inky page is out of the way. Notice the inked brayer sits on the inking slab with its handle on the newspaper.

1.

2.

3.

4.

PROJECTED DESIGN

While the essential qualities of good design do not change, contemporary materials often suggest new and effective ways to relate art activities in the classroom to the art of our times.

Slide making projects, for example, provide the teacher with a practical but exciting means by which to use twentieth-century technology in classroom design. The possibility of projecting their own work, giant-size, often taller than themselves, in brilliant color, makes such activities especially appealing to students. A far cry from the restrictive art problems current in classrooms not too long ago, the inviting prospect of working with attractive materials and contemporary techniques stirs children's imaginations to produce lively, innovative and, often, strikingly beautiful compositions.

Most important, projection techniques provide a first link between the art of the classroom and that of both cinema and television which, together, undeniably comprise the art of our century.

While the dramatic results of slide making are much more exciting and sensational than

1.

2.

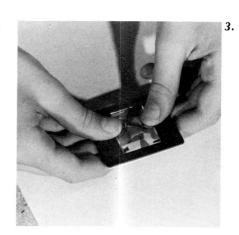
3.

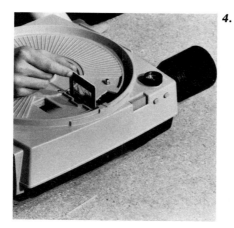
4.

1. *In making a dry slide, a selection of transparent (colored cellophane) and opaque (thread, hair, salt, feathers, netted or meshed materials, wool) materials is arranged on one half of a slide mount. It must be remembered that opaque materials always project black regardless of their color. Overlapping transparent materials will always produce deeper tones or new colors.*

2. *It is best to work on a sheet of white paper both to keep materials clean and to allow transparent colors to show up. Arrange materials on the slide aperture in such a way as to make use of their design potential. Eliminate too thick materials, heavy string, thick cloth because they will interfere with projection.*

3. *When a satisfactory arrangement is arrived at, the slide is closed.*

4. *Now it can be checked in a slide viewer or put straight into the projector. If it is in a plastic holder, the contents can be re-arranged.*

those of most classroom activities, slide-making techniques are not difficult or time consuming and are easily accomplished in the conventional classroom.

Dry Slides

Dry slides are quite spectacular when projected, yet their preparation presents few problems. As all the materials are dry and used in what seem to be almost infinitesimal amounts as compared to other projects, children can work quite comfortably with them at their own desks. Such details of classroom organization as cleanup and display are uncomplicated in this procedure.

Many different kinds and sizes of slide mounts work well for assembling classroom transparencies. Pictured at right is a representative group of mounts popular in schools.

A Kodak cardboard mount that folds along a perforated center line and has one half coated with adhesive. Transparency materials are sandwiched between two squares of acetate, the cardboard halves are closed to hold them in place and gentle heat is applied with a household iron to activate the adhesive and seal the mount (upper left).

A Gepe plastic mount with glass-covered apertures. Clips together without any adhesive to seal in either wet or dry materials. May be opened and clipped together any number of times and may be washed with soap and water or solvents to be used over and over (upper center).

A Pegco "Easymount" slide holder. Acetate rectangles slide into slots in this cardboard mount which hold them firmly in place. Works well for simple transparencies. Is difficult to use with more complicated treatments or with wet materials (upper right).

Glass squares cut to fit 35mm projectors are available at both photo and science supply centers. Slide materials are sandwiched between thin glass surfaces and bound with cellophane tape (lower left).

A bigger version of the 35mm glass slide. Scaled to 3¼ inches by 4 inches for use in the large projectors designed for auditoriums. Only available from science supply houses. Slides mounted in this way can be projected as backgrounds for stage productions and are large enough to look effective when taped to a window (lower center).

A homemade mount cut from shirt cardboard to the same dimensions as the Kodak mount. It is scored along the center line on the outside surface, folded shut to hold the two squares of acetate in place, and bound with cellophane tape (lower right).

Cardboard slide mounts are, as one might expect, always the least expensive with plastic mounts costing the most. Both the plastic and glass holders, however, can be used again and again so that over the long run they are the best investment.

Lifted Slides

Images or textures *lifted* from a magazine illustration can be made to serve as exciting departure points for slide designs. Because the dot pattern basic to magazine printing is magnified when the slide is projected, lifted slides have a slightly unreal quality quite unlike the sharp definition of 35mm transparencies. As such, they invite design experimentation in the way a more defined, self-sufficient image would not. Sandwiching two lifted images or textures in the same slide mount, adding oil and colored ink or bits of colored cellophane will produce odd and fantastic effects that would be impossible to achieve in any other way.

Inexpensive contact *paper is the only additional slide-making material needed to make "lifted" transparencies.*

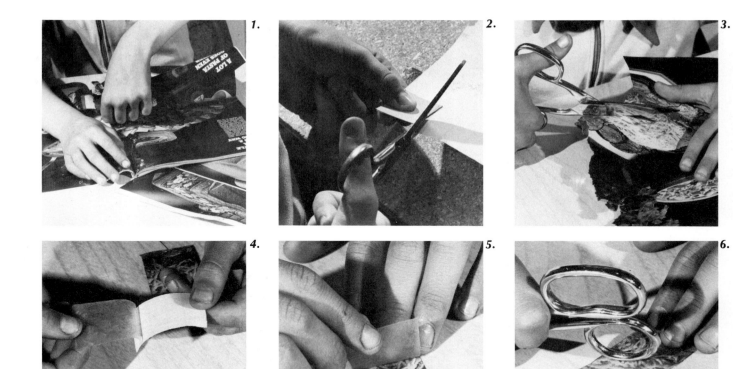

1. The first step in making a lifted slide is to find appropriate visual material. Only magazines that have a slick or glossy surface to their pages are suitable. Distinct colors, design details and single items (eyes, flowers, letters) work best on the tiny dimensions of a slide, approximately 1 inch by 1⅜ inches. Initially, saving pages that contain such material will prove more useful than cutting out individual items.

2. Using a cardboard template a little larger than the slide aperture (1⅝ inches by 1³/₁₆ inches is a good size) as a guide, cut out a rectangle of clear, transparent contact paper for every slide to be made.

3. Cut out a rectangle of magazine paper that looks as if it will project well; once again, using the cardboard template as a guide.

4. Peel off the backing on the contact paper.

5. Adhere the contact paper to the magazine paper with the sticky side facing the material to be projected.

6. Buff the contact paper to ensure a good bond.

7. Soak it in warm water.

8. When the paper is completely saturated, gently pull it away from the contact paper. The paper will fall away but the inks containing the design material will remain fixed to the contact paper.

9. Using thumbs and index fingers and keeping everything wet, roll off any shreds of paper that still cling to the contact paper. This must be done very cautiously as too rough handling will remove the ink as well as the paper.

10. The contact paper can now be sandwiched between the two halves of a slide mount.

11. Then, project or study it in a slide viewer. If the image is not clear enough, the contact paper may need to be resoaked and more paper shreds removed.

12. Now wet or dry materials can be used to enhance the lifted material.

Wet Slides

Wet slides provide one of the most challenging ways for children to experiment with art media. They are based in a technique admittedly messier than that used to make dry slides. But the fact that a slide may be as small as 1 inch by 1⅜ inches means that students can work freely and effectively at their desks or at classroom stations.

Children enjoy this activity. An air of suspense and excitement pervades the making of wet slides unlike that associated with any other art project. Both wet and dry materials are suspended in liquid oil or glue and, no matter how they are initially arranged, their order will be radically changed the moment the slide is clamped shut and its contents squashed together. The excitement continues during projection when bubbles may float haphazardly across a slide as do bits of dry material. Even more sensational events occur when water and Alka Seltzer, liquid soap, or the like are added. Quite literally, one has only to squeeze a wet slide to create a whole new composition.

Children soon learn that these delightfully bizarre occurrences are not altogether unpredictable and so begin to experiment in the best sense of the word. Whatever dramatic or beautiful effects they achieve are amplified as the projector blows each slide up to giant size revealing patterns of crystals, strings of bubbles, and plays of colored light not discernible in the slide itself.

1. Every wet slide needs a fluid base in which the elements of its design are floated. Here a few drops of stand oil *(used in oil painting and available in art stores)* provide the base. Any kind of oil will do as long as it is transparent and viscous. Rubber cement and household cement may also be used. Whatever the base, it can be dripped on one half of the slide mount or applied with a toothpick as illustrated here.

2. As soon as the base is established both wet and dry transparent materials can be added. Transparent colored ink is used here but colored cellophane, vegetable coloring, or dyes will work equally well, each providing a slightly different effect.

3. Opaque dry materials combine in exciting ways with the wet ingredients. Some, like salt *(shown being added here)* and sugar, are interesting because they form crystals or cause the oil to collect in pockets around each grain.

4. Finally, the slide mount is closed and the slide is ready for projection.

1.

2.

3.

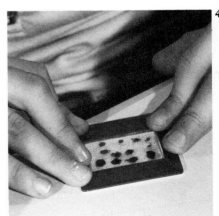

4.

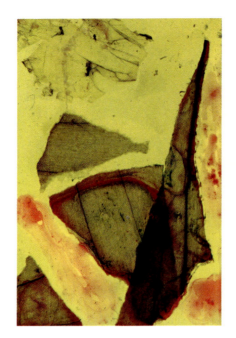

1.

1. A film strip projector adjusted for slides is easy for children to operate on their own.
2. Each projected slide presents the teacher with an opportunity to involve the class in a discussion about a design element it exemplifies especially well; perhaps line or color or texture.
3. While the original slide will measure little more than a square inch, its projected image here is close to seven or eight square feet and could be blown up much larger.
4. A "lifted" slide can be the starting point of an original slide design.

2.

3.

4.

78

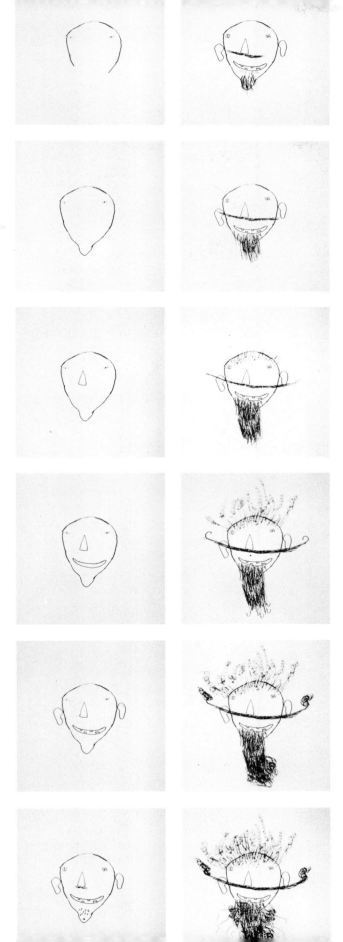

Children are born film makers, and the Super-8 camera is an ideal design "tool" for the elementary school. Not only does the movie camera provide one of the very best ways for children to perceive their environment, but it opens up whole new areas of design involving movement, sound, and time.

Most Super-8 cameras are easy to operate because they are designed for the novice. Whatever special dimension a camera has is always spelled out clearly in the simplest non-technical language in the camera manual which, once again, is written for the amateur. Basic cameras, suitable for the classroom, are surprisingly inexpensive, and today's films surprisingly tolerant of poor lighting conditions and the film maker's miscalculations. Even the cheapest cameras have built in light meters and have either a fixed focus or some device to make focusing easy. Just as with still cameras, often the least expensive is the simplest for the child to operate. In the author's experience many children come from families who own cameras which are used infrequently and may possibly be borrowed for the short duration of a film making project.

There are several basic approaches to film making suitable for the elementary school. Some require more equipment than others but all have a great potential for design. Documentation, drama, animation, and pixilation are four such techniques that will be discussed here. No matter what the technique, children work with film just as they would with wire, clay, paper or paint. First they search out the possibilities of the medium and then use it in terms appropriate to their own enthusiasms and abilities.

Animation is a popular classroom film activity that is a particularly effective vehicle for children's art expression. As it happens, it is also one of the best techniques through which to acquaint youngsters with the fundamentals of film making.

The first film fact the student needs to know in animation is that movie film consists of a

series of pictures or *frames* arranged in a vertical sequence. Each picture is slightly different from the one that follows it. If a person takes off a hat in a movie that gesture will last over a fair number of frames, with the person's hand getting progressively closer to the hat, eventually grasping it, and then moving it away from the head. If you look at the series of frames on page 79 you can see how a fifth grader at Collegiate School in New York City constructed just such an animation sequence. Film passes through the projector at 18 or 24 frames a second. Frames in such a sequence are projected so quickly, one after another, that the illusion of movement is created; and we accept the fact that the beard is actually growing! In actuality, we are seeing a series of still pictures, but our eyes are not quick enough to distinguish one frame from the next.

To attempt animation in the classroom, the following equipment is required: a Super-8 camera with film, a tripod, and two photoflood bulbs with reflectors. Attach the camera to the tripod.

Spread a sheet of newspaper on the floor and elevate the camera. At the same time focus it until the area you see through the viewfinder is sufficient for your needs and the print appears sharp and well defined. Judge or measure the distance from the camera lens to the newspaper and check with the manual to see if, in fact, the camera can be in focus at that distance. If not, move the camera higher. When the elevation and focus are satisfactory, place a light on either side of the camera and check to see what the built-in light meter registers. If it signifies that the light is too intense, move the lights back; if there is not enough light, move them closer. Make sure there are no shadows where the animation material is placed. With some of the recently developed high speed films, lights may not be needed if the photography is done near windows or outside. Some teachers advocate placing a square of inexpensive synthetic black velvet at the base of the tripod on which animation materials can be arranged; the black absorbs excess light and provides a neutral border in case the focus is too wide and the camera shoots beyond the art work. Once everything is set up, it is well to mark the position of the tripod legs with masking tape. For a second shooting session, everything can then be quickly slipped into place.

Several types of animation lend themselves to the elementary classroom. *Progressive drawing,* as indicated in the sequence on page 79, requires that a sheet of drawing paper is taped down in camera position. A drawing or painting is then completed step-by-step, the camera records each phase of the sequence, frame by frame. Some cameras have built-in single framing controls; others do not. Shoot four frames either by using the control button, or a remote control cable, or merely by pressing the exposure button. Let the student or students doing the art add one more small detail, shoot again, and so on. Be careful that while all this is going on, the camera never changes position and nothing is moved that might cast a shadow across the shooting area. This same technique may be used to shoot sequences involving cut paper, collage materials, and illustrative matter from magazines. The camera can be mounted to shoot horizontally, and clay or plasticine sequences can be shot against painted backgrounds.

Pixilation is a similar technique to animation in which actual objects or the students themselves comprise the art elements. It is sometimes called "stop-action" photography because that is actually what is involved. In pixilation, sequence shots are taken at 4 frames for every "episode" to give such illusions as a piece of bread skittling across a table and jumping into a toaster. To create such an effect, 4 shots would be taken of the bread, the slice would be moved an inch or two, 4 more shots would be taken and so on until the sequence ended. In this technique, the tripod should stay fixed but the head is loosened so that the camera can be *panned*. Children never fail to enjoy pixilation immensely. They never fail to be delighted as they watch themselves on the screen speeding around the playground as if by magic, appearing and disappearing, and involving themselves in hi-jinks that are hilarious on the screen.

Documentation involves a much more normal use of the camera than do animation and pixilation. Here the camera is often handheld and a normal speed of 18 frames per second replaces stop-action camera work. While animation techniques conserve footage because of frame-by-frame shooting, documentation consumes film at a much more rapid rate and shooting sessions need to be carefully planned. There are few technical problems in documentation although students do need to be cautioned about focus, panning too rapidly and camera wobble. Experience indicates that it is necessary to convince students at the elementary level to limit their themes. Topics such as *Signs* or *Circles* that focus attention on specific areas are much more likely to succeed than more expansive ones such as *The City* or *America*.

Using the same techniques as in documentation, but adding a story line involving *drama*, can be a very rewarding extension of the normal classroom art program. Designing costumes, backgrounds, props, and titles, and working with sound and make-up are all very exciting to the elementary student and stimulating incentives for creative work.

Extensive background experience in film and advanced knowledge of its techniques are not necessary for the teacher who wants to attempt using film with students. Having an enthusiasm for children, teachers make better film instructors than experts whose interest is in the medium. Film can be *edited in the camera*, for example, when editing and splicing skills and equipment are not available. Cameras, projectors, and film at the Super-8 level are designed for use by beginners.

However, film is an expensive medium. It is worthwhile to explore its many possibilities through the now extensive literature on classroom film making to ensure that footage is used economically and profitably and by taking advantage of the many sources of community support available.

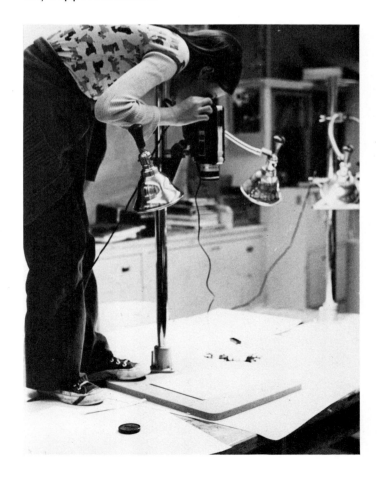

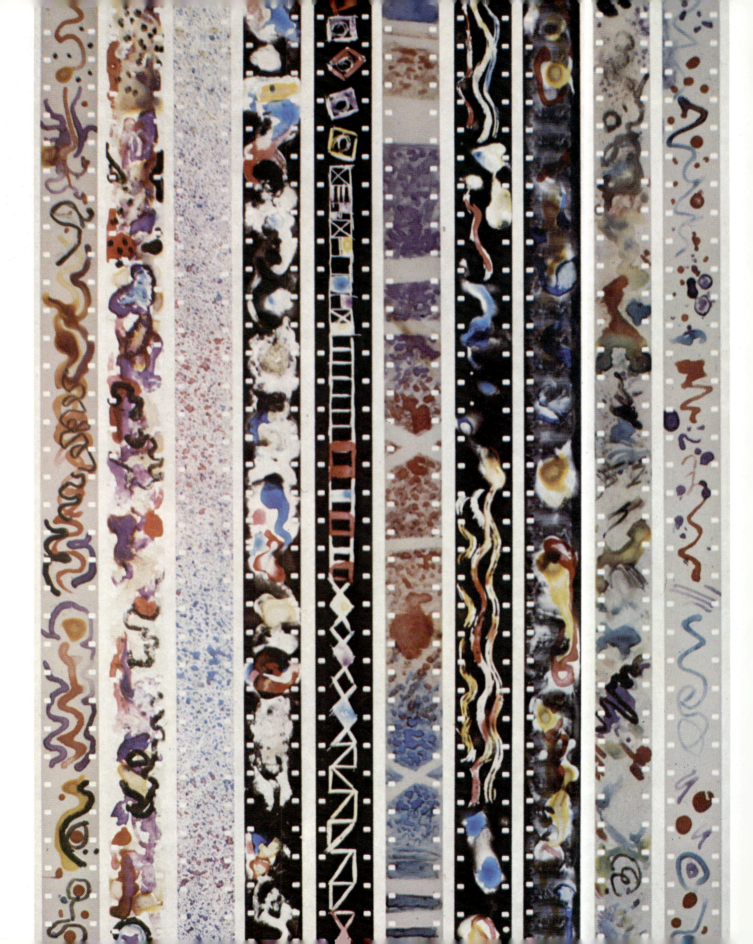

Design Experimentation with 16mm Leader

Working with regular 16mm film in the same manner as is possible with Super-8 film is economically out of the question for most schools. Inexpensive 16mm *leader,* however, lends itself to dramatically exciting uses in the classroom. Leader is untreated film not intended for projection but especially prepared for attaching to the beginning and end of a movie to facilitate viewing and editing. The kinds of leader that hold most promise for design are clear leader, white coated leader, and black leader. Discarded 16mm movie film that has been exposed and printed is useful, too; but white leader that is plastic throughout is opaque and should be avoided.

With only easily obtained art materials and without the use of a camera, films such as those on page 82 are not difficult to make. Attractive in themselves, they are unbelievably entertaining and beautiful when projected. Involvement in such direct and down-to-earth film making is a good way to introduce children to the first principles of animation and the appreciation of films at many levels.

Making a film without a camera is such an uncomplicated procedure that it presents few problems for the teacher. Because of its exciting results and the fun of its group involvement, it is always popular with students. Although the techniques involved are disarmingly simple, this type of film making opens up a whole new area for design, that of design in motion. Such a technique was virtually unexplored in classrooms only a few years back.

a. *Marker designs on clear 16mm leader.*

b. *Colored ink blotted with colored ink designs superimposed, plus scratching on clear leader.*

c. *Marker designs with colored ink designs superimposed on clear leader.*

d. *Colored ink splattered (using a toothbrush and knife blade) with India ink and colored ink designs superimposed on clear leader.*

a.

b.

c.

d.

1. *Because felt-tipped markers and colored inks spot badly, surfaces to be used for film experimentation need to be stain proof or well protected. The film should be fastened down (with narrow strips of masking tape) emulsion side (dull side) up with ample loops where the film turns back on itself. The film should be left intact with the tail attached to the reel to ensure that it will be rolled back right side up.*

2. *When students work with black leader, Q-tips dipped in a mild laundry bleach will eat away the emulsion to reveal the clear base beneath. Discarded 16mm movies can be worked on in this way, too, with remnants of the original images being allowed to peek through the design. Anything that has a sharp point or even a moderately sharp edge – scissors, compasses, straightened-out paper clips, hairpins, nails, pocket knives – will be effective in removing emulsion in a controlled manner.*

3. *Scratched or eaten away areas can be colored with markers and colored inks. Test out coloring materials ahead of time as some markers, particularly water-based ones, will not adhere to the film base and some colored inks, acetate inks, for example, are opaque. Materials that pile up on the film or tend to peel off can cause trouble by clogging the film gate of your projector.*

1.

2.

84

e. Scratching plus use of a hole puncher with marker and colored ink rubbed into surface of black 16mm leader.

f. Black leader, emulsion eaten away with laundry bleach, with colored inks superimposed.

g. Exposed 16mm movie film (notice clown's head), emulsion eaten away by laundry bleach, with colored inks plus press type letters superimposed.

4. Markers and colored inks work well on clear leader, too. Care should be taken to see that designs are continuous with a repetition of symbols and effects, as individual designs flash by so quickly in the projector that they are hardly noticed.

5. Before the tapes are removed and the film readied for the projector, the loops left when it was fastened down will need attention, as will the uncolored strips that indicate where the strips of masking tape were placed.

6. When the film is eventually ready to be shown, the projector should be set to "silent" and the speed turned to 18 frames per second. It is worthwhile to extend your experimentation with sound. Curiously, almost any sound tape or record with a fast tempo will provide a good accompaniment for a 16mm experimental film. Interesting sound tracks can be produced by using percussion instruments, different tape speeds, "found" sounds, and collages of bits and pieces from a variety of records.

e.

f.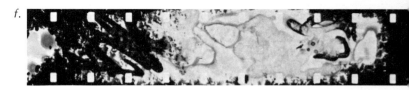

g.

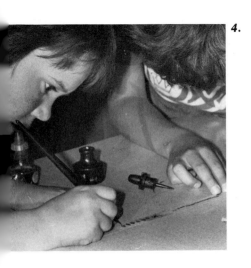

4.

5.

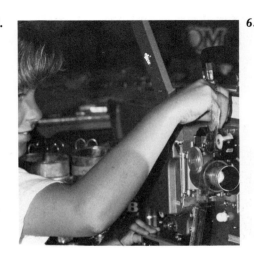

6.

MURAL MAKING IN A DIFFERENT WAY

Group projects in which children have an opportunity to share ideas and work toward group-inspired goals should be an integral part of every school program. Unfortunately, when classroom facilities are not geared to large-scale undertakings, activities meaningful to the social development of the child are often avoided. Here is a mural-making project, however, which provides the basis for a most rewarding group experience and lends itself to even the most restrictive classroom situation.

In this activity, the class is divided into work groups of several children each, the number depending on the size of the mural to be attempted. After each group has finished its initial planning and has completed the first steps of the process, students can work independently at their own desks while still forwarding the aims of the group. Eventually, everyone comes together again to reassemble the mural which, in the course of the project, has been cut up into design areas. The advantage of this technique over some traditional approaches is that here every child, regardless of drawing skills, plays an important role in both the conception and completion of the mural. Because most of the activity takes place at individual desks or work tables it can be creative and group-oriented while, at the same time, adaptable to a normal classroom.

So that the vigorous and spontaneous quality of this kind of mural making may be maintained, it is necessary for each child to work independently for that stage of the process where individuals are solely responsible for their own sections of the mural. Then, as no one knows what the total mural will look like until the last section is taped into position, there is an excited air of expectancy to this project. Children find this immensely stimulating so that their interest is maintained at a high level throughout the activity.

A 24-inch or 36-inch wide strip of Kraft paper is adequate as a mural surface. However, a mural of this type will be much more effective if strips of Kraft paper are glued together (as in the mural we see here) to make an over-all surface to fit a pre-determined space. Loops of masking tape can be adhered to the back of the

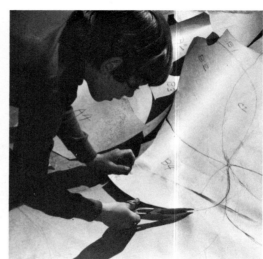

completed mural. Then the mural is pressed against the wall surface so that a true mural effect is achieved.

An appealing way to break up the back of a mural into design areas is by the use of a *snap cord*. Take a long length of sturdy string and have two students, one at each end, hold it taut while a third runs a piece of chalk along its length. When the string is saturated with chalk dust, have the two students stretch it across the mural, tight against the paper. Let the third student snap it to leave a perfectly straight, sharp line wherever it touches the surface. Repeat this until the back of the mural is crisscrossed with chalk lines that form a series of closed areas. Code the areas and cut up the mural so that it achieves the same random effect when the parts are taped into position as in the original technique.

Although the mural we see being assembled here is non-objective, the technique lends itself to the portrayal of realistic content. If a lifelike theme is contemplated, the procedure is much the same. Whatever the realistic material may be, it is drawn on the front of a sheet of Kraft paper which serves as the mural surface. Simplified forms are suggested. Although some detail will stand up well, shading and fussy treatments are best avoided. When the drawing is complete, an abstract design in a similar style to the one shown here is drawn on the back. The areas created by this design are coded and the mural cut up.

The pieces are distributed to individual students to be colored. As in the original mural, students must not reveal how they are treating the areas of the mural assigned to them. Although the drawing may be realistic, obviously the color scheme cannot. When all the sections are colored, they are assembled by use of the code and pieced together with masking tape to complete the mural. Murals evolved in this way turn out to be quite successful and can be strikingly dramatic.

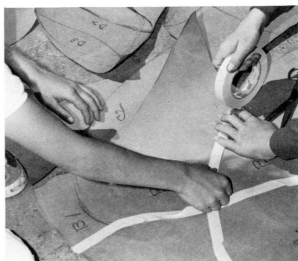

DESIGNS THAT GROW

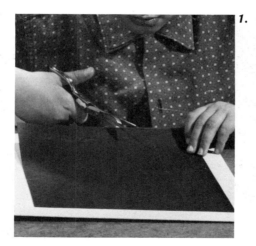

1. Each student begins his design with two sheets of construction paper in contrasting colors. One sheet is larger than the other and acts as a base.

2. Shapes are cut without pencil lines from the smaller sheet.

3. Each of these designs has "grown" from a single sheet of construction paper on a larger background to the interesting compositions shown here.

4. These shapes are moved out and away from the center so that the resulting design begins to cover the background.

5. After the general layout of the composition is decided upon, some parts of it may be cut into even more interesting shapes.

6. When all the shapes are cut and satisfactorily arranged, they are pasted into place.

90

 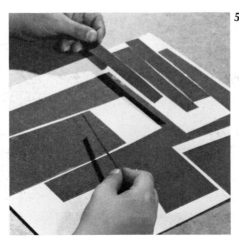 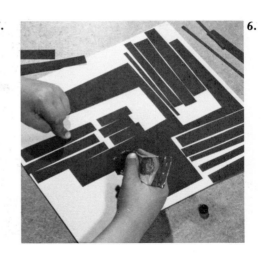

When introducing a design activity, the classroom teacher must give serious thought as to how to get the class started on the project and then how to keep twenty-five or thirty students moving ahead, more or less in pace with one another, towards its successful completion.

The initial step in this design activity is so conducive to creative work and so readily understood by children that it determines the success of the total project. It is characteristic of activities that are effective in what we have come to accept as normal-sized classes because it is built around a strategy in which the class stays together for the first two or three steps. The teacher works with the entire group until students are sure of themselves. Then they begin to develop their own original ideas and the teacher is free to concentrate on helping individuals.

Each child begins with two pieces of construction paper in contrasting colors. Cut ahead of time by the teacher on a paper cutter, the smaller sheet should leave a border of from one-half to three-quarters of an inch on every side when placed on the larger sheet. The students must cut the smaller sheet into design shapes then move them out in all directions to create a composition filling the area of the larger sheet. It is best to have one or two students demonstrate how they would do this. Have them point out how, by cutting and moving pieces of the smaller sheet, the color of the larger one becomes part of the design.

It takes only the cutting and moving of one shape for children to see the inventive possibilities of this design activity. In no time, they are cutting shape after shape and manipulating them into effective arrangements. Their designs literally *grow* before their eyes!

Although the examples shown here are 14 inches by 14 inches, children can create giant designs along similar lines with equal ease and with as much success. These large designs make striking school decorations.

Activities such as this, which make use of simple media and uncomplicated procedures, provide children with an enthusiasm for good design. They introduce students in a non-academic way to the mechanics of design, in this case, the use of negative and positive shapes, that provide valuable background when they are ready to attempt more advanced techniques. The design *sense* which they develop is sure to be reflected in even the most diverse art activities.

BLUEPRINTING

Some of the most effective activities in contemporary art education make use of traditional techniques to achieve their objectives. In such cases, it is not an understanding of the procedure which is of greatest importance but the uses to which it is put. Blueprinting, long a favorite school process, holds a richer potential for design construction than may at first be realized. Experimenting with its possibilities may reveal many new avenues for creative discovery.

Unusually beautiful compositions can be created simply by arranging cut paper shapes on the blueprint surface. Overlapping paper shapes plus the sharp linear definition of lengths of string or thread add another dimension. The incorporation of nature forms, unusual textures, and found objects, such as keys, paper clips, elastic bands, help to enrich compositions.

Materials can be placed on the blueprint paper for a short period of time in the sunlight or for a much longer period under bright electric light. For complicated compositions, materials may be held in place by a sheet of glass, as were those in the design shown here. Materials useful in either approach include ferns, grasses, leaves, buckram, cheesecloth, excelsior, netted materials, cellophane, and different weights of tissues and papers.

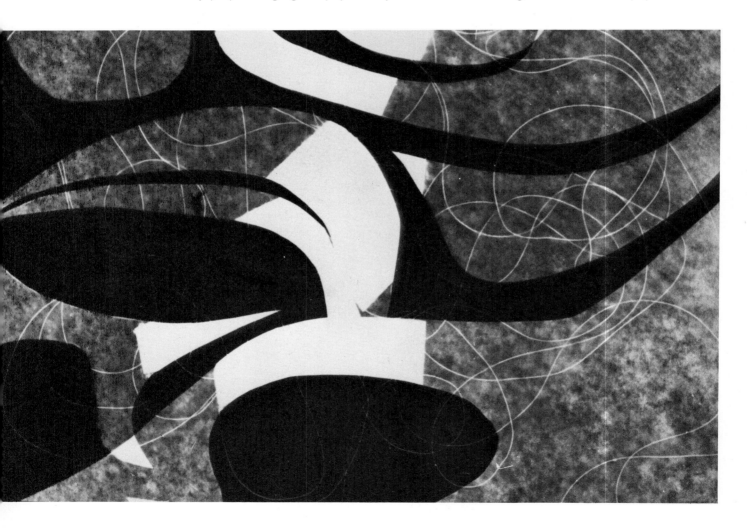

1.

2.

3.

4.

1. To make blueprint designs, students must first get together the materials they want to incorporate in their compositions. They can use nature materials, found objects, or cut paper shapes (as is the student pictured here). Thread, string, and yarn are useful when a line quality seems indicated.

2. When an arrangement has been decided upon, the student, working in a dim light, should assemble it on a sheet of blueprint paper. As soon as it is ready, the composition may be exposed to the sunlight for a very short period or to a light source such as a photoflood bulb for a much longer time. The actual time can be determined by observing the change of color of the blueprint paper. Here the composition plus the blueprint paper were shielded from the light by a double fold of opaque drawing paper.

3. Everything was taken into the playground and the drawing paper was opened up to expose the blueprint composition to the direct sunlight.

4. When the unshielded areas of the blueprint paper begin to turn grey, the composition has registered and is ready for developing. Now it can be presoaked in water or placed directly in a bath of room temperature tap water to which a few drops of hydrogen peroxide have been added. In no time, the design emerges in the sparkling whites and brilliant blues characteristic of the blueprint process. The print, which is permanently fixed, can be dried between the pages of a newspaper.

WEAVING A DESIGN

The best way to gain a knowledge of and sensitivity toward materials is to work with them. The project illustrated here demonstrates how an adaptation of the traditional craft of weaving can make children aware of the nature of fabrics. In this activity, children develop an understanding of the structure of a fabric by building a rudimentary loom and by actually weaving. In addition, they arrive at a number of art decisions involving the physical characteristics of string, wool, yarn, cloth, natural and synthetic fibers, leather, and appropriate found materials.

Designs created in this manner are invariably handsome and inventive. Yet all materials needed can be easily gleaned from family and classroom scrap boxes, and the looms can be made from discarded cardboard. While the act of weaving is the central activity, children also benefit from the practice of exercising discrimination and imagination in their choices of appropriate colors and textures.

Such activities have a double significance for children; they introduce children to the craft of weaving through uncomplicated procedures and make them aware of the creative and aesthetic potential in weaving that is usually associated with such arts as painting and sculpture. For one child, classroom weaving may be the beginnings of a lifelong interest in the craft as a means of personal expression; for another, it may awaken a lasting enthusiasm for the beauty of well-designed and expertly crafted fabrics.

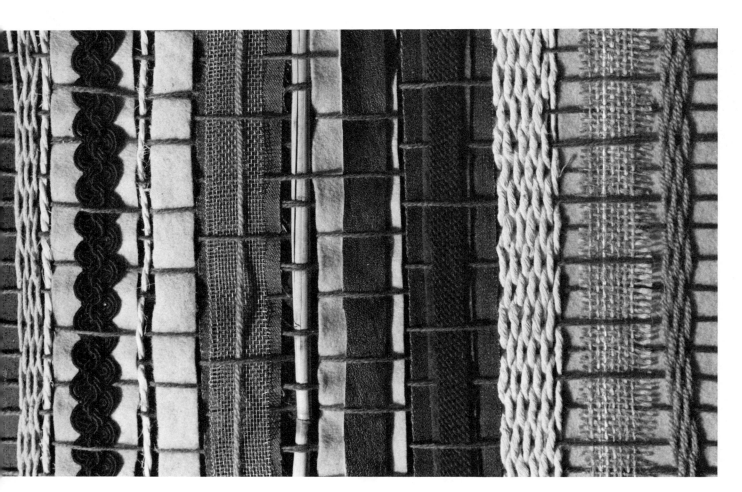

94

1.

2.

3.

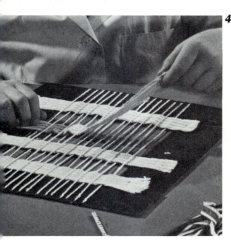

4.

5.

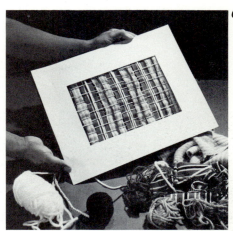

6.

1. *To weave a design the student must first construct a simple loom. In this case four strips of stiff cardboard are stapled together to form a rectangle (a sheet of heavy cardboard would work just as well). An equal number of ½ inch slits are cut in the top and bottom edges of the rectangle to accommodate the warp which will eventually support the woven design.*

2. *Then coarse string (wool, yarn, cord would do) is used to form the warp, looped around the teeth (made by the slits) and pulled not too tightly to lay flat against the front of the loom.*

3. *Here is the back of the loom. Notice how the string has been looped around the teeth with its two loose ends taped down.*

4. *Yarns and materials from the class scrap box can be used to create the woof which is woven through the warp at right angles to it. As the object is to weave a design rather than a piece of cloth, both yarn and strips of material are pressed into service at this point.*

5. *Some pipe cleaners are woven across on top of the strips of material to add variety. As each new element is added, its ends are stapled to the two outside edges of the cardboard loom.*

6. *When the weaving is complete, a cardboard frame is placed over it to hide the raw edges of the weaving and give the design a finished look.*

CLAY MODELING

The plastic qualities of clay appeal to children. These qualities allow them to push it in, pull it out, squeeze it, add parts to one another, and make a thing one moment and destroy it the next. Yet, clay has qualities which can frustrate them when they attempt to work with it, such as the tendency to dry out and crack and its inability to support itself when moist. While children should be encouraged to work freely and exercise originality they should also be helped to recognize the limitations of the medium so that they can avoid disappointments.

Clay commercially prepared for classroom use is just the right consistency for modeling. This consistency is not stable, however. If children are permitted to work with it too long, the clay will dry out, crack, and be difficult to handle. If water is used in the modeling process, the clay will become soft and sticky; and cracks will appear when it dries.

In general, children work with clay in one of two ways. Some build up their models by adding pieces to make a whole, as is the sixth grader we see working here. Others pull out single parts from the whole. Most children tend to be inclined strongly one way or the other but do not hesitate to use a combination of both methods to achieve their goals. Children must be allowed to work in ways most natural to them; step-by-step stereotyped approaches to clay sculpture contribute nothing toward helping children find themselves as creative individuals.

Although the student pictured here works toward realism in his sculpture, his feeling for design is evident in his placement of the parts of the figure and the decorative treatment of the cowboy's clothes and equipment. Because children can manipulate clay with ease and can draw into its surface effortlessly, it makes a fine design medium for the elementary school.

Uncomplicated art activities with modest objectives, and those based in simple media, often provide richer opportunities for children to design freely and creatively than more pretentious projects. The sculpture activity demonstrated here, for instance, is uncomplicated in concept, scrap cardboard being its only component. Yet it offers students an unrestricted opportunity to creatively develop ideas while manipulating the material out of which their sculpture will grow.

Fundamentally, the method used consists of fitting pieces of cardboard together by the simple expedient of cutting a slit in one piece and slipping the edge of the adjoining one into it. Uncomplicated as this procedure is, it makes for an endless variety of different sculptural forms and allows children the freedom to constantly readjust their structures, fitting pieces together first this way, then that until a pleasing aesthetic effect is achieved. When the final result is arrived at, a spot of glue at each joint makes the sculpture permanent.

BUILDING CLASSROOM SCULPTURE

Children should be encouraged to look at their projects from all sides as they work, and to be cautious that the "architecture" of their structures is clean cut and economical, not heavy and tedious. Variety can be introduced by using a hole puncher, as demonstrated here, by applying color, or by working with contrasting types of cardboard, for example, a smooth surfaced board with a corrugated cardboard.

The illustration on page 100 is a Xerox print of a collage made from a few strips of burlap, some mesh of the kind used for vegetable sacks, kernels of rice, and a few lengths of reed glued to a sheet of white cardboard. It took some time to gather the material and, of course, time and effort to assemble the collage; but the actual printing process was almost instantaneous. Although the collage materials were fastened to cardboard for convenience, they could have been assembled right on the glass of the Xerox machine.

Copy machines, such as the Xerox, reproduce the image of anything that is not of an exaggerated thickness. None of the messiness of the traditional printmaking processes is involved and, of course, none of the problems associated with materials that do not take ink readily or that smudge and blot. This means that children have a great deal of freedom in making up their Xerox compositions. This kind of printmaking does have limitations, however. For example, while fabrics with pronounced or open weaves will yield sharp, modeled images; materials that are solid or too pale may not reproduce well at all. Some machines, too, reproduce newspaper and magazine illustrations with excellent clarity, while others return clouded and spotty copies of such material. Although most school machines have copying beds of a generous depth, others can only process art work that is flat. As with all design processes, only experimentation will indicate the boundaries of creativity with Xerography.

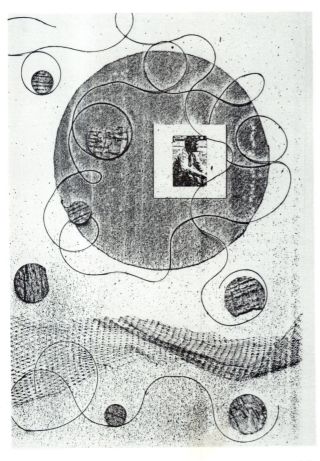

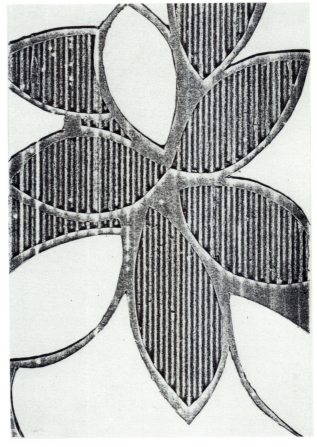

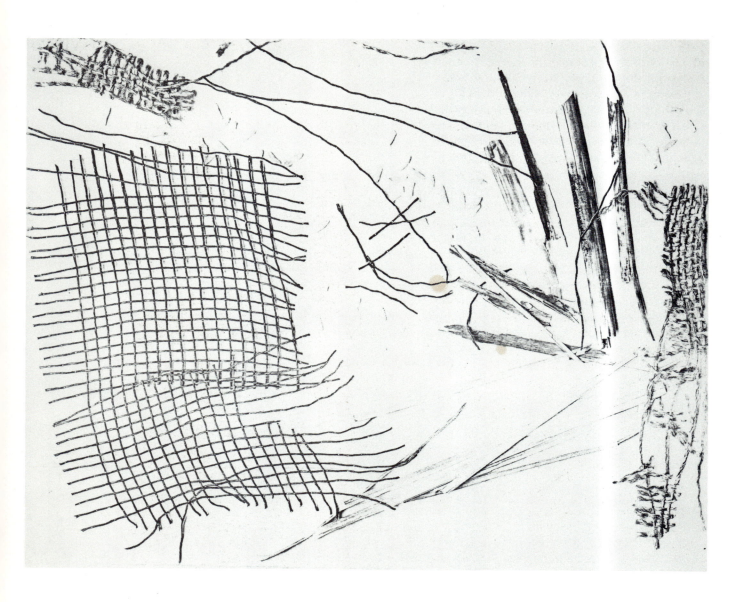

Xerography works equally well in copying collages composed of material cut from magazines as it does with collages made from real materials. By reducing everything, including color, to precise black and white tones, school Xerox machines give unity to compositions that might otherwise not look as well organized. Xeroxing, too, replaces the pasted-up appearance of the original collage with a printed look in which there is no evidence of paste or rubber cement. Prints from both types of collage lend themselves to further enrichment with crayons or colored pencils and inks.

100

Most design activities are centered in a process, a technique, or a material which in each case establishes its distinctive character. While each activity is a satisfying entity in itself, it often shares its identity with a group of other activities which are *extensions* or *spin-offs* of itself. Because of this it is not difficult to develop a new activity merely by adding or changing a material or altering a process. For example, in cardboard printing, if we retain cardboard as the printing base (as on page 64) but substitute string as the design element (see this page), or perhaps a found material (see page 102), rather than a second layer of cardboard as in the original version, we retain the process but create a new activity. Similarly, by adding plaster of Paris to clay (see page 102) we develop a carving medium out of the modeling material that characterized the activity demonstrated on page 96.

Such reconstituted activities are effective in class. Once students understand and develop considerable facility with the original process, they work confidently and enthusiastically on its extension, often inventing variations of their own.

Seeking out extensions of basic processes which have proven successful in class instead of constantly shopping for new ideas is a productive approach to program planning in design. Developing extensions establishes a certain constancy of purpose and encourages a full use of specialized equipment and supplies.

NEW PROJECTS FROM BASIC ACTIVITIES

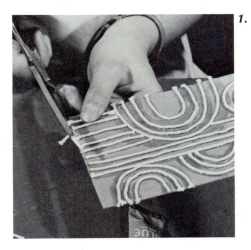

1.

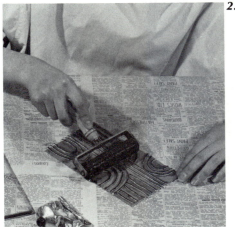

2.

3.

String Printing

1. *String is glued to a backing of stiff cardboard.*
2. *Water-based ink is rolled onto the string design with a rubber roller.*
3. *The inked design is placed inked side down on a sheet of paper and printed in the same manner as a cardboard print.*

Collage Printing

1. *Collage materials are glued to a sheet of stiff cardboard. Lace is used here but materials like burlap, corrugated cardboard, cork and netted fabrics would work as well.*
2. *Water-based ink is rolled on the collage design.*
3. *The design is printed as if it were a cardboard print.*

Clay Carving

1. *Just enough water is added to a dry mixture of 4 parts clay powder and 2 parts plaster of Paris to make a thick liquid of the consistency of heavy cream. Other materials, such as paint powder and vermiculite, could be added to the basic mix. The mixture is poured into a waxed milk container and left to warm up and then cool.*

2. *When the medium has set but is not yet hard, it is removed from the container and carved with a pocket knife or a paring knife.*
3. *The carved form is allowed to dry. Now the surface can be roughened with files and rough sandpaper in some areas and smoothed with fine sandpaper and steel wool in others.*

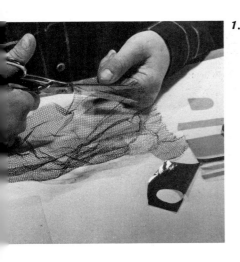

1.

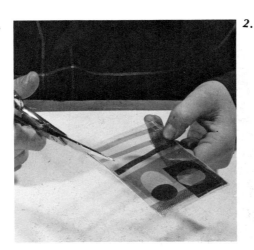

2.

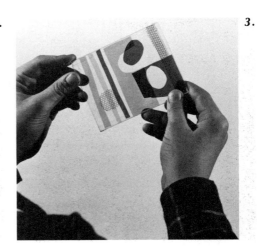

3.

Transparencies

1. Cut two 3¼ x 4 inch rectangles of medium-weight clear acetate to fit a large slide projector.* Combine opaque materials such as threads, net, feathers, lace with transparent cellophane shapes. Glues, inks, and oil can be added as in making 35mm slides.

2. Bind the "slide" together with clear cellophane tape. Trim off the ends of the tape. Now the design contents are firmly sandwiched between the sheets of acetate.

3. The slide can now be projected. If a projector is not available, cut a 3⅛ inch x 3⅞ inch aperture in a sheet of black construction paper large enough to cover the glass surface of an overhead projector. Project slides by placing them over this opening.

*More expensive 3¼ inch x 4 inch glass slides can be purchased from some photo dealers and science equipment houses. These, of course, can be used over and over again.

BIBLIOGRAPHY

Background:
Churchill, Angiola. *Art for Preadolescents.* New York: McGraw-Hill Book Company, 1970.

Gaitskell, Charles D. and Hurwitz, Al. *Children and Their Art,* 3rd ed. New York: Harcourt Brace Jovanovich, 1975.

Greenberg, Pearl. *Art and Ideas for Young People.* New York: Van Nostrand Reinhold Company, 1970.

_____ *Children's Experiences in Art.* New York: Reinhold Book Corporation, 1966.

Guyler, Vivian Varney. *Design in Nature.* Worcester, Mass.: Davis Publications, 1970.

McIlhany, Sterling. *Art as Design: Design as Art.* New York: Van Nostrand Reinhold Company, 1970.

Montgomery, Chandler. *Art for Teachers of Children,* 2nd ed. Columbus, Ohio: Charles E. Merrill Company, 1973.

Elements of Art and Design:
Davis Publications, Inc., Printers Bldg., Worcester, Mass. 01608.
  Concepts of Design, Gerald F. Brommer, ed. A series of ten volumes to do with the principles and elements of art and design.

Van Nostrand Reinhold Company, 450 West 33rd St., New York, N.Y. 10001.
  Reinhold Visual Series, John Lidstone, Stanley T. Lewis and Sheldon Brody, eds. A series of ten portfolios each containing 24 18'' x 24'' prints. A teachers manual is included with each portfolio.

Design Activities:
Belvin, Marjorie Elliott. *Design Through Discovery.* New York: Holt, Rinehart and Winston, 1970.

Cooke, Robert W. *Designing with Light on Paper and Film.* Worcester, Mass.: Davis Publications, 1969.

Erickson, I. *Print Making Without a Press.* New York: Reinhold Book Corporation, 1966.

Horn, George F. and Smith, Grace Sands. *Experiencing Art in the Elementary School.* Worcester, Mass.: Davis Publications, 1971.

Lidstone, John. *Self-Expression in Classroom Art.* Worcester, Mass.: Davis Publications, 1967.

_____ *Building with Wire.* New York: Van Nostrand Reinhold Company, 1972.

_____ and Bunch, Clarence. *Working Big.* New York: Van Nostrand Reinhold Company, 1975.

_____ and MacIntosh, Donald. *Children as Film Makers.* New York: Van Nostrand Reinhold Company, 1970.

Lord, Lois. *Collage and Construction,* rev. Worcester, Mass.: Davis Publications, 1970.

Rainey, Sarita. *Weaving Without a Loom.* Worcester, Mass.: Davis Publications, 1966.

Russell, H. R. *Small Worlds.* Boston: Little, Brown and Co., 1972.

Wilson, F. *What It Feels Like To Be a Building.* New York: Reinhold Book Corporation, 1968.

Special Publications:
Greenberg, Pearl, ed., *Art Education: Elementary.* Washington, D.C.: National Art Education Association, 1972.

Rice, Susan and Mukerji, Rose, eds., *Children Are Centers for Understanding Media.* Washington, D.C.: Association for Childhood Education International, 1973.

The Reinhold Book of Art and Craft Techniques. Originally published in Germany in ten separate volumes under the title "Basteln mit Kindern." New York: Van Nostrand Reinhold Book Company, 1976.